DIRTY DADDY

DIRTY DADDY

The Chronicles of a Family Man
Turned Filthy Comedian

BOB SAGET

itbooks

AN IMPRINT OF HARPERCOLLINS PUBLISHERS

FIRST EDITION

Designed by Lorie Pagnozzi

Library of Congress Cataloging-in-Publication Data has been applied for.

ISBN 978-0-06-227478-6

14 15 16 17 18   OV/RRD   10 9 8 7 6 5 4 3 2 1

For my brilliant and understanding daughters

CONTENTS

INTRODUCTION

WE ARE WHAT WE ARE

As a kid I often heard from my mom, as well as from the teachers in every school I attended, that I needed to behave myself and watch how I spoke. Apparently I was a mischievous little bastard. By the time I started out in stand-up at seventeen, I was careful about my language; this helped me get on television shows and go on the road opening for musicians like Frankie Valli and the Four Seasons and Kenny Loggins.

But one day in my early twenties, I snapped. I didn't want to disappoint my mom, but I couldn't take the censorship of it all. Some of the comedians who fascinated me the most—Lenny Bruce, George Carlin, and Richard Pryor—had also felt oppressed by the things you could and couldn't say in public.

On Conan O'Brien's show he once asked me how I was able to keep it together through my eight years on *Full House* and not say the wrong things in front of all the child actors. I explained that I would occasionally lose it while we were shooting and arbitrarily yell out things like "Cock! Shit! Fuck!"

It was a planned "bleep," a setup so Conan could ask me on the air something he's always asked me on his show: "*What* is the matter with you?"

We were being funny with that exchange, but there's a deeper truth behind it. It's why people go into a life of comedy in the first place. When you're told not to do something, unfortunately, for some of us, is exactly when you do it. No means no. But not to a comedian.

In my career I've had the fortune of being able to work continually in radically diverse creative worlds. By day I've done some of the most family-friendly TV imaginable. Then, often in the same day, I've gone onstage in the L.A. comedy clubs and whirled off with an adolescent's delight about my grandma's projectile diarrhea.

That in itself could, by many psychiatrists' standards, be a bit of a call for help. I never do it to shock anyone, even though people have sometimes thought of me as a shock comic. If it is a through-line or a constant to what I do, it's not something I'm proud of. But I'm not ashamed of it either. It's more of a handicap. Or, depending on your perspective, a gift. It's what I used to think of as my mania. Now I've come to embrace it. You have to love yourself. But not in a movie theater, because they will tabloid your ass.

Mostly I've just always done what I found funny, strange as it may seem. Immature taboo humor (*good* immature taboo humor) always made me laugh. I love all kinds of humor, but my love of "sick silliness" started with my dad—whom you'll hear a lot more about—and his constant dick jokes. He was a grown-up who said things a nine-year-old like me always wanted to say *because* I was told not to.

Joking has also been a means for me to avoid pain. I've lost a lot of people, and throughout my childhood—almost every two years—someone in my family died at an unnaturally young age. The more tragedy befell us, the more odd gallows humor I would release. My humor, especially once I started doing it professionally, was always dark and twisted. Like your penis if you accidentally slammed it in the door of a car.

This book is about how that humor helped me survive. It's been inside me for a long time. It has congealed. I am writing what comes out of me. Well, not exactly, or this would be a book about "leakage."

The goal of living a full life is so, at its end, you'll have learned some things along the journey. I'm nowhere near the end yet, but I've already had some incredible experiences. I've met and worked with some amazing people, I've lived, I've loved, I've cried . . . and through it all, I did it my way. In this book I'll talk about many of the people I've known in my life and in the worlds of comedy and entertainment. Some of them are still around; many are not.

I've had some dark times, but the thing about dark times is there *has* to be light at the end of the tunnel. And one great thing about being a man is you can go to bed depressed and feeling negative, but when you wake up in the morning, through no effort of your own, you've got a nice display of morning wood to let you know it's the start of a new day. You could be waking up next to the love of your life, or the girl your buddy told you not to talk to the night before because she was a drunken evil vortex. Or you could be totally alone in bed and not sure if you want to get up yet—but *he's* up. Like a sundial catching the first ray of morning light, casting its shadow on your stomach. Or if you have a tiny penis, casting its shadow directly next to itself, hardly a shadow at all. Or if you have a choad, which I'm told is a penis that is wider than it is long, and you were hoping to use it as a sundial but only had, say, an inch of length to it . . . you could still be proud to look at that tiny stump of wood in the middle of the day and declare to the universe, "It's one o'cock!"

No matter what the size of your penis, what matters most is not size, it's honesty, and yes, I'm switching to deep sincerity, that's right, from penis size to what really matters in life . . . the stuff a lot of people take for granted: health, family, friends, human kindness, a love for all living things, and being honest and true.

"Honesty," as Billy Joel says, "is such a lonely word." And I don't think he's referring to honesty in regard to penis size—unless yours is truly gigantic, in which case, if you are a compassionate man, have you ever thought of being a donor? Like when you fill out your driver's license form and sign off your organs to science, you could hypothetically, if they allowed it, leave your penis to someone who could use the extra inch-age. "I'd like to leave my lungs to the American Lung Association and my penis to Marcus, an eighteen-year-old man who awkwardly wanted to talk to me once at a urinal in the Phoenix airport."

As you can see, I have a tough time writing too many words in a row without a dick joke thrown in. Or a shit joke. Or a combination of the two, which you shouldn't do, because as all the great philosophers say, "You can get an infection."

My fear at this point is that this book will not be taken seriously, or for some, it may be taken too literally. If the latter is the case, I recommend you see a shrink. I know there are readers of this who probably don't normally read books; they are fans of comedy. I would be remorseful if seventeen-year-old boys who have read just this introduction so far have already turned the book into a drinking game—taking a shot every time the word *penis* is mentioned. For the safety of those young people, whom I have huge concern for, as they are our future, I'd like to hereby change the drinking game cue word to *shart*—a hybrid word (*shit* + *fart*), which sadly secures no points in Words with Friends.

You will come across an ample amount of sharting in the chapters that follow. Maybe not as many as you will penises. But that just means you won't get quite as drunk. Sharting, as a term at least, is relatively new, but penises have been around forever, and penis humor is what my dad and various other weird mentors in my life imparted upon me as a way of dealing with all of life's pain and challenges.

When I say humor has helped me survive, I don't mean survival in terms of, say, the Holocaust. Nor in terms of getting stuck in a mountain chasm and having to cut your own arm off in order to stay alive. And for sure this book is not about surviving in the way our reality-TV culture portrays it.

If you are reading this, it means you are a survivor too—you have survived the first pages of a book by me. I am honored you have chosen to spend some of your precious time doing so, and in the following chapters I will share with you my stories of humor, inspiration, and uncontrollable sloppy loud flatulence, if that's where your entertainment nut lies.

Personally, my entertainment nut lies to the side, underneath my laptop as I type this. And to be honest, that is not an easy position to be in. I had no idea writing a book would involve so much pain. The pain of my nut—in fact, both of them—being heated under my hard drive. Odd it's called a hard drive considering I am flaccid while I write. Well, usually.

It's cool to me that it takes so long to write a book. My only concern is that as I type my hard drive may heat up and start making that sound like teeth grinding. I'm not worried about the hard drive; I'm worried that after the many months it will take to write this book, the sound will be actually coming from my testicles. That they could possibly be eating themselves. A very wise man once said, "Eat thyself." Okay, no wise man ever said that. I doubt anyone ever said that. And if they had been able to say that, they wouldn't have been able to hear it because they were munching on themselves. Baron von Munchimself.

I apologize. I don't want to open by dwelling on lascivious stream-of-consciousness adolescent ramblings. So I'll return to them shortly. You may want to sit down for this. Or put on a gimp suit, zip it up all the way, and have your Dominant strap you into a recliner and read it to you in its entirety while occasionally feeding you Top Ramen noodles so your blood sugar doesn't drop. I must have you in top physical condition while you are ingesting this material.

Chapter 1

A LIFE OF FREE ASSOCIATION

Before I dive in, I should give you a heads-up that my book, like my life, does not always proceed in a linear fashion. When I write—whether it be stand-up, or scripts, or graffiti on the sides of a high school, or a Sharpie self-portrait on a biker's ass—I enjoy free-associating, just hitting on any subject that somehow pops into my mind. Underpants. I don't give a thought to how the synapses fire. Deviated septum. I enjoy it, like riffing in my stand-up. Detached retina. It's a skill of mine that is fun to employ. Like performing improvisational jazz must be for musical people. Come to think of it, there are probably a lot of jazz musicians with detached retinas. For them, I will record this book on tape with pure conviction.

So yeah, my writing and thinking are not very linear. Polyp. Neither is my life in general. Barium. I'm going to pop back and forth in time a lot in this book. I'll try to not get too *Cloud Atlas*'y on your ass, but just stick with me. Events happen to us every day that jolt us back to an earlier time, to a nightmarish moment from high school or a poignant memory of our parents.

When I started in stand-up at a very young age, I was even more into free association and random word combos. My material at the time was often dark and came from the fact that I moved a lot as a kid. The first ten minutes of material I wrote, when I was seventeen—which I also used on my first talk-show appearances, such as *The Merv Griffin Show*—started like this: "I have no friends and I have no life and I live in a moped. My mother is Gumby and my father is Pokey and I'm Mr. Potato Head."

Comedians' first ten minutes usually stay with them the first several years of their career. It's their mission statement. Their disclaimer that lets people know who they are. Or were. It's also a good time to make fun of your name if you have a funny or strange one. My last name rhymed with some obvious words. Woohoo. In a way, it's a good thing for a comedian to just have the worst last name possible: "Ladies and gentlemen, please welcome . . . Jimmy Uterus." You would never have to ask him where he's from.

When I see or hear my stuff from back then, I can't believe how manic my style was. Always irreverent and fast-paced. Too fast, like I was running from something. Which I was. My childhood. [*Sound effects: record screech*]

So I guess that's where I should begin this book, with a few moments from my childhood that seemed to form the comedy person I eventually became. It was a long time ago but I sometimes still feel like a kid, even though I know all too well I'm not one anymore. I know this because I'll occasionally wake up in the middle of the night and find one of my toes has broken off under the sheets in the corner of the bed. Age does things to a man's body parts. Sometimes I'll put a couple of my broken-off toes on ice with Bacardi, lie back in my Barcalounger, and watch *So You Think*

You Can Dance. (Shouldn't that show have put a question mark at the end of the title?)

When I was a kid, my mother told me, "When you grow up, not everyone is going to like you." And I told her, "I need names." Well, I have them now. I have a list. But I can't use all of the people's real names in this book because they will come after me and castrate me. And I need my balls because I am still a relatively young man. In my head, a very young man.

In fact, this may be overly personal, but one of my testicles is younger than the other. I came out right ball first and it dragged the second one out minutes later. My left ball is always posturing to my right ball because he knows he's younger, so he likes to rub it in my right ball's face. Sometimes, and this may be superstitious on my part, they rub against each other, and it brings me luck. A few times, I've come into money this way.

All balls aside, rethinking it, perhaps it is okay for me to mention some of the names of people in this book if they are now deceased, as long as I attempt to speak of them respectfully. My intention is only to bring up people who seemed to like me. Shorter list. I've met so many remarkable people so far, coming up through stand-up all these years, who just aren't alive anymore. Because they are dead. Some really great people who helped change my life and career, people like Richard Pryor, Sam Kinison, Rodney Dangerfield, Johnny Carson.

And those are just some iconic comedy names I'm dropping. In my personal life, I've lost some of my true heroes, my closest people: my two sisters, four uncles, my dad, many friends, and a goat my father bought for two *zuzim*, which translates into half a *shekel*, an unheard-of good deal for a goat those days. My father bought that goat for the family but it proved to like my mother better than him, always headbutting my dad's ass and yelling, "Maahaaa."

In this day and age, if a person in a civilized place were to go to the market and buy a live goat and take it home, they might not be taking it home to *eat it*, if you know what I mean. That's right, there are some sick goat fuckers out there. You read about it every day. Well, probably not *every* day. But I guess you could read about it every day if you set your Google alert to "sick goat fuckers." But I wouldn't suggest doing that if you aren't one.

Richard Bach, author of *Jonathan Livingston Seagull*, once wrote, "If you love someone, set them free; if they come back, they're yours, if they don't, they never were." But what if you're one of those people who set their Google Alert to "sick goat fuckers"? What then? Sure, you may be all by yourself in the yard crying out loud, "But I love Daisy so much, why did I listen to Richard Bach? I miss my Daisy!" Shame on you, on your knees, weeping like a little girl all alone in a field over a *goat*! If that's you, I'm here to tell you: Stop it! That's one of God's creatures. Let it be with its own kind. You go and get yourself some cheap therapy at a nearby clinic and start looking for someone more like yourself—a human. Something without cloven hooves.

Sorry about that digression. See what I mean? That's a typical demon of mine. Not a bad demon, if there's such a distinction, just a fallback to deal with hurt. As soon as I go into a dark subject, like discussing the people I've loved and lost, I off-road into absurdist comedy perversion. It's both a means of protection and a kind of denial, a blessing and a curse. Wait, it's not a blessing at all. I guess it would be a bad habit and a curse. Some people spout clichés for no reason, just because it's how we're trained by society. "Look for the silver lining," a lovely and hopeful cliché. But some things don't have a silver lining.

At least that one's better than "It was meant to be." That's what someone says after something terrible happens, as a way of rationalizing or making themselves feel better. That crane fell off that forty-story building and landed on Aunt Betty because it was "meant to be." So it was preordained the day Aunt Betty was born, from their point of view, that at some time in her life a giant crane would fall off the roof and crush her flat? And that's okay, because it was meant to be? I don't look at life that way. I think things just happen to people. That's healthier, I feel, than believing there's some grand scheme where your story is already inscribed in the Book of Life. Books get rewritten. This one definitely got rewritten and this is *still* what I wound up with. I'm looking up at this moment, making sure there are no cranes in sight.

George Carlin was so eloquent in pointing out clichés . . . "He's out walkin' the streets. You hear this when a murderer gets paroled from prison. Guy'll say: 'Now, instead of being in prison, this guy is out walkin' the streets.' How do we know? Maybe he's home watching TV."

George was very kind to me when I moved to L.A. in 1978 when I was twenty-two. Always asked me how it was going, asked me if I "saw the light at the end of the tunnel."

"Yeah," I said, "but it's connected to a train headed straight for me." I was so depressed for so many years over trying to become a working comedian that my sense of self-worth would plummet . . . I'd go from being the kid with the dream, positive he was going to be the biggest comedy star ever, to a young man who feared *he* was going to wind up that guy paroled from prison "out walkin' the streets."

George knew the journey of show business, and he knew about following your own voice, no matter what the cost—but more significantly, he knew that the life of a comedian is about survival. Succeeding as a comic isn't just about writing some funny stuff, or having a good comedic persona, or getting lucky and winding up with a TV or movie career. It's about being a survivor. Going into it for the long haul. George was more prolific than just about anyone I've ever seen. Much like Chris Rock and Louis C.K., who follow in his path (metaphorically) with their hard-core work ethic of writing and developing fresh material. They're part of the new Mount Rushmore of Comedy.

At the time that I am writing this, my newest stand-up television special is behind me, my first in five years—and I found the experience profoundly rewarding. But that significantly pales in comparison to George, who did *fourteen* HBO specials starting in 1977 until his death in 2008.

He was a philosopher. And if you listen to his "stuff," it's the highest level of the form. He had a lot to say. And he said it. I wish he'd had a chance to say more. After I appeared in *The Aristocrats,* in which George was the Obi-Wan Kenobi, I reached out to him to go to lunch. I'd been paid high compliments by a couple people he was close to about how he dug my stuff. He knew how hard it was to reinvent oneself—from family TV to the kind of adult humor that made me laugh, then back to family TV, while continuing to spin what I found funny in my stand-up.

Anyway, the end of the George story is obviously sad. He passed away shortly after we were trying to schedule lunch. I think he wanted to avoid having lunch with me so badly that he chose death. My narcissistically self-deprecating cap to the loss of one of the many great people I knew briefly (in his case, very briefly) in my life whose end came too soon.

There were many others. My family saw so much death and drama over the years it was like we were always waiting for the next tragedy to arrive. As soon as the first of my young uncles died, the other ones got paranoid—as some Philadelphia people of the Jewish persuasion do—that they were "next." And unfortunately, they were.

I always found it a paradox that when I was growing up in Norfolk, Virginia—this was before moving back to Philadelphia, where I was born—people would occasionally ask my family, "Are you of the Jewish persuasion?" That is a statement of redundancy. If you are Jewish, odds are it is within your nature to be persuasive. Better, I guess, than if the expression had been "Are you of the pushy Jewish variety?"

But my theory is this: Pushy people became that way because they were afraid they'd get left behind. Because when they were kids and all the food was put out, they were the last ones to get to the buffet, so they didn't get any. And as they got older, they could relate more to their parents' lives—in essence, always running from the guard at the border. This was all the more reason for them to charge ahead and get some roast beef brisket before missing the opportunity of nabbing the juiciest slices. It all comes down to survival. And a good piece of meat. But we'll get to that.

Rodney Dangerfield used to tell me his whole life was like the Jewish man trying to escape Europe during the war, and he had to give the Nazi border guard his best six minutes so the guard wouldn't shoot him dead. That's how Rodney looked at life. You're only as good as your last six minutes. It's not just a *set*—it's a choice between life and death. Comedy is serious business.

Whenever you talk to people about your survival, it makes them want to share their own losses with you. It's like comparing battle scars. Makes me think of that scene in *Jaws*—which I just watched for maybe the tenth time—with the great Robert Shaw, Richard Dreyfuss, and Roy Scheider, where they compare their wounds at sea.

A shark attack is similar to my sweet aunt Ruthie grabbing my face and kissing me so hard she sucks blood to my cheek. In fact, her ex-husband, my dad's brother, my uncle Joe, resembled Roy Scheider . . .

And not unlike Robert Shaw in *Jaws,* he was also bitten in half—except by his ex-wife. Uh, okay, Bob. And by the way, I love my Aunt Ruthie, which means more slams to come.

Uncle Joe survived but I lost three childhood heroes to heart attacks; all were funny, handsome overachievers with high cholesterol, and all died between the ages of thirty-seven and forty-one. First, when I was eight, I lost my uncle Ozzie, one of my dad's three younger brothers. He was only forty. He had a heart attack while running down the street chasing a couple kids who had stolen his tire. Nice, right? They tell me I look the most like him.

One year later, I lost my uncle Manny to a double heart attack.

Apparently, he had two different heart attacks—one brought on by his business, the other just by pressure in general. His wife, my aunt Millie, loved him more than anything, but she was young and a bit of a hottie—and with that comes complexity. Yes, I just typed that my late aunt was a "hottie." I'd like to believe she'd have smiled at that one.

Manny was found after his double heart attack on the couch in the living room; he was later diagnosed as having had a front and back heart attack (to use clinical-speak). As for my aunt Millie, may she rest in peace and God bless her—as we say before we dish someone—she was known to have complained to him constantly about the state of their lives, before, during, and I'm guessing *after* the heart attacks. She meant well though. I'm still close to her daughter, my cousin Sandra. Life can certainly be complex. This is true for most people if you get to live long enough. I feel for anyone reading this who presently knows of no sadness or stress—you may be in for a shock. Jesus, I hope I'm not the one to break it to you with this book.

You look at someone as amazing as Stephen Hawking, one of the greatest minds of our time, and as I write pieces of my family's history I think about what he's been through. Just imagine, he's never had the privilege of saying what drunken guys say to each other in bars all the time: "I wouldn't kick *her* out of bed." Because he couldn't. Has this book been pulled out of the display windows in airports yet?

Getting back to my family, the death toll kept rising. A couple years after we lost Manny, even more tragically, Manny and Millie's twenty-one-year-old daughter, Bonnie, succumbed to cancer.

Then, six years later, when I was fifteen, my dad's youngest brother, thirty-seven-year-old Sammy, died of a heart attack while playing tennis. I guess if you were to pick which one of all these heart attacks you'd want to have, you'd choose the one during tennis. At least you're all in white, teed up for the great U.S. Open in heaven. God was just watching Sammy play tennis that day, trying to keep score, and said to himself, "Thirty–love-to-have-him-up-here-in-heaven." It was what it was. Sucked.

Just for clarification, when I mention God watching Sammy play tennis, I'm using poetic license, not referring to the Carlin-esque version of an almighty being with a long white beard, pulling numbers out of a hat, deciding who shall live and who shall die. That's far from my view of religion. I'm more of a spiritual believer. It doesn't make sense that an all-powerful wise old man would just make a decision on a whim and take my handsome thirty-seven-year-old uncle from this earth.

It does make sense, however, that an all-powerful old *woman* would make that happen. I don't know why we never picture God as an old woman. That's right, I'm suggesting that my innocent, handsome uncle was playing tennis and an old lady with a white beard looked down upon him and said with a Betty White–ish cackle, "Look at that young piece of tail prance around on that tennis court; I think I'll add him to my collection." And in an instant he was gone.

I don't believe that either, of course. I don't see God as a man or a woman but as a giant transgender Jabba the Hutt creature with striped faux fur. Maybe God looks like Rick Ross.

It was this demented pseudocreative mind of mine and my father's that helped us deal with losing my uncles at such young ages. All these men were my childhood heroes. Sammy especially. He wanted to go into show business. He could sing, he was handsome, and he was the baby of five brothers and a sister, so he believed he could do anything. He also had the first PhotoGray transitional lenses I'd ever seen. He was the coolest.

He and my aunt Barbara lived on the Main Line in Philly. She was also cool, equally talented, and she still is. She's alive and is still "the shit"—in the nicest possible definition of that term. She and my uncle Sammy loved their upper-class hippie ways. Just looking at photos of them back in the day makes me want to put on a double-breasted suit and tinted glasses and smoke hemp.

After Sammy died, Barbara married Lee, whom on occasion she has smoked pot with for over forty years. I don't know if that's totally true, but they assured me they wouldn't sue me if I printed that. I'm also very close with Barbara's daughter, my first cousin Allison. She's one of my dearest friends and has always, since her father's death, wanted to get the most out of life. I want to go on record that I'm not *saying* she's a smoker of the weed. I'm typing it.

Pot doesn't really agree with me, but it always did with many of my relatives and friends. Rodney Dangerfield swore by it. And on it.

Here I go bouncing back and forth again. Sometimes there's been a thin line between my blood family and my comedy family. I started to feel related to comedians as I got older—it's like we share some sort of comedic DNA—but before that it was all about my uncles.

My uncle Joe, the one who *didn't* die young, was cool too. He lived longer than my dad's three other brothers, but he did lose one testicle due to cancer. And in retrospect, due to divorce. She metaphorically got one of his balls in the settlement. I also got divorced once, but I was fortunate, I had a good lawyer—got to keep both of my balls. Thank you, Universe.

Still, my balls have been the source of many lifelong issues. You'd think that the problems men have, when they stray or act out of sexual impulsivity, are caused by their dawg-like quality of following the divining rod that is their penis. But no, it is my belief that the root of the problem lies at the root of the penis—the balls. They fill with fluid, which must find a way to leave the body and enter the atmosphere.

Fundamentalists would say it's for procreation, but the physical act of the expulsion of the male fluids usually doesn't involve another human being. I have a doctor who says ejaculating once a day can improve cardiovascular health. But so does walking up stairs. I do both. I ejaculate as I walk up stairs. That can be dangerous if on the way back down you slip on your own semen and tumble to your death. That definitely isn't something you want to hear on the news after the coroner's report.

But severe leakage can also *save* your life, if you are kidnapped and they are able to find you by the long trail of leakage you leave from, say, your backyard to the kidnapper's hideout.

Sorry, that was cheesy to bring up. As are my testicles right now, because, truth be known, I am still typing this on my laptop, and when you have a computer on your lap, the fan in it has no ventilation; it's smothered by your crotch. If I had the choice, that's the way I'd like to leave this world, smothered by your crotch. And I don't even know you. My crotch is so smothered right now that I have decided to name my testicles—the Smothers Brothers. Okay, I will not.

When I set out to write this book, I was concerned I would fill it with too many dick jokes. That is no longer my concern. I can now note that it is full of testicle anecdotes. That's the only indication that I am a more mature man now than I used to be. Penis references become outweighed by testicle references. Gravity creates maturity.

Anyway, back to my uncle Joe and his balls. I loved him a lot. My aunt got only half his balls, not half his heart. The last days I got to spend with him, he was lying in hospice and watching Tiger Woods win the U.S. Open in 2008. He was so happy to watch Tiger's comeback. That's what my whole family of that generation was based on—an unrelenting work ethic and comebacks.

According to people I've talked to who have interviewed me, I've had many comebacks myself. I prefer to call them do-overs. Or redefinings. Or I say what a lot of people with long careers that change over time say about themselves when asked, "Where have you been?": "I never left."

I suppose I got that . . . whatever you want to call it—survival instinct, elasticity?—from my elders. Some of them are still around. Besides my interesting and incredibly strong brick house of a loving mother, Dolly—whom I'll talk more about in the next chapter—I am also fortunate to have still living my aunt Thelma, who is also my godmother. I always called her "Aunt Temi."

She's very sweet and always wore beautiful glasses. Then she had Lasik. I miss those glasses. Hers were the kind you want your aunt to have—the ones that appear to be upside down, made of platinum and glass that is not from this world but rather from the mesmerizing prisms of Planet Krypton.

Her husband, my uncle Jonah, whom I also love immensely, has giant glasses himself that frame his face with a statement for all: "I'm ready for welding." I saw him once without his glasses and it scared me. It was like seeing Peter Parker without his Spider-Man suit. Although Peter Parker didn't look any more macho *in* his Spider-Man suit. By the way, I wore one of those Spider-Man suits on TV once and it really accentuates the peanut.

My dad—whom you'll meet in the next chapter—had a similar head-accoutrements situation. He was also blinged out in huge glasses and had a large nose (yes, I got a direct hit of that gene) and a strange, Zorro-like pencil-thin mustache that started just under his nose and ended abruptly above the top of his two wafer-thin lips. I never saw my dad without the mustache, but I did also see him once without his glasses.

I was about sixteen, and when I walked into my parents' bedroom (not something you ever want to do) my dad turned over and his glasses were off. I could have sworn his nose and mustache had been erased. He looked like one of those aliens from *Mars Attacks!*, without the glass helmet to protect his sensitive nonfeatures. I even recall a quick glance to his nightstand, where I thought I saw the entire set of facial features lying there as one unit—glasses, nose, mustache, even eyebrows attached.

At that instant I was fearful my own father was the actual Mr. Potato Head. The first thing that went through my mind was "And he didn't make a penny off all that merchandising."

Ironically, years later, it was my dear friend Don Rickles who said that line. He's kind of a father to me now that my dad's been gone for several years—and Don *is* the actual voice of Mr. Potato Head in the *Toy Story* movies. All right, that last line was not so much ironic as just name-dropper-y at a time when I had nowhere else to go with this story. Point is, my dad's face was diminished without his huge glasses resting on his gigantic nose, and I was scared to see him without his headgear at two in the morning.

The only other time I was thrown like that was when I walked in on my mom one day and she was dressed as Gimli from *The Lord of the Rings*.

Deep apologies to my mom; of course that never happened. She never wore a helmet. Once, in a television stand-up appearance on HBO, I mentioned that my mother used to wear a Viking helmet and culottes. That didn't make her happy. So as I mention it here, in this book that will be in print, I'd like to apologize to my mother for saying she used to wear a Viking helmet and culottes. I might have also mentioned "tit plates" at one time on some show, and for that I apologize to my mother as well.

And so this book has begun. Tales of tit plates, tales of comedy, tales of loss, tales of tail . . . that are not spoken of. Okay, for those of who you are waiting for me to talk dirt or tell out-of-school stories, I'm planning to, once I clean my emotional plate, in like seventy or eighty more pages . . . Wait, I can't do that, there are people's lives at stake here, and sharing personal secrets about them serves no purpose. Except for this one time when I met this girl . . . No, I'm not going to do it. And anyway, she was a "woman." Least that's what I told the judge. And she was in big-girl pants and everything.

For now, dear reader, I hope you are curling up in bed with someone you enjoy reading with—because you've been together so long there's just nothing more to say to each other—and if this book is working for you on any level—occasionally one of you is laughing out loud, so the person next to you may actually speak to you and say, "What are you laughing at?" And you may say, "Well, it's in reference to Bob's penis when the light hits it just right."

And with that, I am now going to roll up my sleeves as well as my pant legs, put an ice pack on my lap, and move on. Now may be a good time to get a beverage.

Chapter 2

DEATH AND COMEDY ARE CLOSELY RELATED

It sucks when funny people die. It sucks when unfunny people die too, but not as much. As you now know, many of my relatives died young. Many of them were funny. But none was as funny as my dad, who passed away in 2006. Of all my childhood heroes, biggest of all was my father. Well, there was this other guy, a UPS driver who picked me up after school one day and took me to the cornfield. No, that didn't happen. He was a FedEx guy. Reset.

My dad, Ben, was a huge influence on my doing what I do: hitting on young women . . . last deflection, I promise, what I meant to say was . . . working in comedy. The only young woman my dad ever hit on was my mother, whom he started dating when she was sixteen. He was seven years older than her. And ironically seven inches taller than her. On his back. (Don't worry, I have it all figured out: when I give my mom a copy of this book, I will just white out a ton of shit.)

My dad taught me nothing means more than the primary relationships in our lives. The love of a great woman and children. Hopefully your own, not the neighbor's. And then what matters almost as much is the love of good friends. Just make sure you bring in enough income to buy all their love.

Like me, my dad dealt with death and all the hardships in life through humor. Sick and weird humor. We would be standing next to an ice machine and hear a cycle of ice drop with a loud thud, and he would say, "There's your grandmother." As though her corpse wanted to say hello by dropping its two hundred pounds within earshot. Not always funny, but always some kind of metaphysical release from the pain.

I think of him now and it all makes sense. He was such a good father and such a great man. I still don't understand the mustache though. He would darken it with an eyebrow pencil for that perverted Zorro look. But instead of leaving Zs, he just left weird shit in your room. One night when I was seventeen, I drove home late and he had put an eggplant under my sheets, propped up on the pillow with a towel wrapped around it like Yentl in a babushka, with a note next to it that said, "Bob, I waited up for you."

He could have been a stand-up, if he wasn't a child of the Great Depression who had to raise his five siblings by going into the supermarket meat business. He was truly a survivor. His work ethic stayed with me my whole life. He drove himself hard for fifty years—worked his way up from a butcher in a supermarket to become a VP of meat. That's right, a vice president of meat. I don't know who the president of meat was at the time, but I do know my dad was under a lot of pressure from work. Meat weighed heavily on his mind. His meat pulled him down.

No, that's not a setup for a joke. But when I was about six, my world was pulled down when my dad had a massive heart attack himself. He used to smoke six packs of cigarettes a day. Didn't even open them, just put a box of Camels in his mouth and torched 'em. It was like *Mad Men* except it wasn't about the world of advertising. It was all about . . . wait for it . . . meat.

He really did smoke six packs of Camels a day, from the moment he got up till the moment he put the lights out. Crazy. Next to the surgeon general's warning on cigarettes they should've added his picture. It would've been the actual size of his head. He had a very small head. His head was about the size of the surgeon general's warning on the side of a box of cigarettes, to be specific.

He had a second heart attack six months later that damn near killed him. He was in a hospital in Norfolk, Virginia, and I remember that my mom, Dolly, claimed she *had* to become his nurse because she didn't like the care he was being given. But years later he informed me that my mom had decided to take over the nursing duties because his actual nurse had "fallen in love with" him while sponge-bathing him back to health.

He spoke of it proudly, telling me his nurse had said, "You can't die, I am in love with you," and describing to me in detail how she had tried to bathe him back to life. Ech. He was good at grossing me out. Great news was, he didn't die, and my mom had the nurse removed from the case.

The nurse's story had an unhappy ending. As I recall, she was fired from the hospital entirely, but who knows—my entire family history is a blur when told by the surviving elders. It's frustrating; just when someone is ready to tell you their life history, their mind starts to go, and the facts become diffused. I'm glad I'm starting this book now.

The thing about my dad is, as much of an influence as he was on me, I didn't really get to know him as a person until I was about sixteen. I guess he was shy. Processing it now, I realize he didn't relate well to young kids. I think he was very relieved when I finally got old enough to understand a good dick joke. I had two older sisters, so once my father had a son [*angelic musical fanfare played here*] he figured he could just talk to me like I was already the beer-drinkin' buddy he'd been waiting for his entire life. Again, I was sixteen.

Some of my favorite times were earlier when I was almost a teenager and he would take me on road trips from Norfolk (where we lived from when I was maybe four, or seven; I don't know the year because my mother changes it each time we discuss it) to Richmond, Virginia, to visit "the stores"—the other branches of his employer, the way-bankrupt-and-gone Food Fair Stores, a company that was run by some Mr. Potter–like individuals. My dad wasn't Willy Loman. He was a good and noble man. More like George Bailey, one of Jimmy Stewart's best characters. George Bailey was a fictional man who believed in justice and kindness. And he, like my dad, believed that a man should be paid fairly for his efforts. Which meant he got fucked.

So I was about eleven or twelve when he drove me to Richmond. First, we checked out "the stores" and then we checked out the competition, which was A&P or Stop & Shop. One time he told me Stop & Shop was going to merge with A&P and be called Stop & Pee. I don't know what to tell you except that he was my dad. And he was a great dad and a great man. And I loved him. Creepy jokes and all.

So on this one trip we were at a store and we went to the back to check out his rival's meat case. Dad looked closely at all their self-service meat, all individually wrapped in plastic. My uncle Jonah claimed at my dad's funeral that it was my father, Ben Saget, who helped bring to the American supermarket the whole concept of "self-service" meats—of not having to go to the butcher anymore and get your steaks wrapped in paper. I know that can't be true, but I do believe my dad was heavily motivated to make self-service meats the thing of the future.

As he led me up and down the meat case, he'd try to impress upon me how amazing it was that all these meats just sat in the case, fresh, prewrapped, and preweighed with a sticker that told you everything you needed to know about your purchase. I'm telling you this story because I did something that day that I feel bad about still. As my dad strolled past the case checking out his rival's wares, I poked a hole with my finger through every package I could, on a mission to ruin all their self-service meat so that customers would be outraged by the perishing, unsuccessfully Cryovac-ed raw product decomposing in front of them.

We got into my dad's car and were about to drive off when I proudly exclaimed to him what I'd done. "Dad, I poked a hole in every one of those packages of meat. No one will want to buy their meat and they'll have to go back to Food Fair, where there are no holes poked in their packages."

I'll never forget how upset my dad was: "Why did you do that? You shouldn't have done that, son. I have to go back in there and straighten this out." That was the moral compass of my dad. Probably not the best business move to go back into that store, find the meat manager, and confront him with what his numbskull son had just done to his entire display. But he did it anyway.

I was confused. I had thought I'd been helping him. He got back in the car fifteen minutes later and wasn't mad at me, just told me never to do it again. He said every man was entitled to be in business and it was wrong to sabotage others just because they're your competition. And then he let it go, and we continued our father-son day trip.

He took me to the deli he'd been talking about the whole time on our two-hour drive to Richmond. We both ordered a particular sandwich there that single-handedly set me on a path of bad deli food I am still trying to eradicate from my diet. The sandwich was called [*timpani drum roll*] "the Sailor Sandwich." I was eleven or twelve when I ate it, but I finally passed it just last month.

I'm proud to say, having been a deli clerk myself and a past member of the Amalgamated Meat Cutters' union (I've been on a leave of absence since college), that I understand the value of the girth of a good hunk of meat—not to mention the metaphoric penis humor that springs from it. Okay, you may want to sit down or go online for this . . . the Sailor Sandwich consisted of rye bread with melted Swiss and of course fatty pastrami (redundant), sauerkraut, and a huge Hebrew National knockwurst grilled and split as its centerpiece.

How, you ask, could my dad have possibly had two heart attacks several years earlier, eaten that crazy food, and lived until eighty-nine years old? Answer: luck, meds, he didn't want to die, and he loved a good piece of flounder. He was one of the first people on

Coumadin, a blood thinner that's commonly used now. In those years they didn't have Lipitor, which is what I now take daily—okay, hourly. (If you're reading this book, I assume you have high cholesterol or will shortly, I'm flinching as I type this; and I'm relatively sure I know what I'm talking about.) Doctors have told me for years that once you turn forty you should take Lipitor. I'm not trying to get free Lipitor (or the generic) by mentioning it here. I just want to keep *you* alive.

That's one of the things I love about myself—I actually want to keep people alive. As long as they can stay alive. I mean, life's a window of time we're given; why not open it and stay inside it as long as we can, right?

Sorry I typed the word *right* with a question mark at the end of it. I look forward to the day when people have dropped *right* and *really* from our vernacular. But damn, I've used it a lot in this book. Whatever. Oh, and can we drop the *whatever* too? And while we're at it, can we get rid of "That's what *I'm* talkin' about!" Oh wait, no, let's not get rid of that—that's the name of my last comedy special. Slid that in so quietly, right? Damn.

Well, it's all just words anyway. Personally, words and names don't really hurt me. Because my father passed on to me the last name of Saget, I would say as a kid I was pretty much set up in the area of name-calling. Saget came from a Russian Jewish name that kept changing, probably because my ancestors kept running from persecution and name changes were all a person could do to hide their identity back then. Now we have nose jobs, Botox, and caramel-apple-headed orange-hued face-lifts. But back in the day, there were no plastic surgeons, so a name change and a wig were about all you could do to hide from the enemy.

I heard Ivan the Terrible was a victim of a bad plastic surgeon. When the bandages came off, the doctor looked at him and said, "Ivan, you look terrible." Wikipedia has this to say about Ivan the Terrible: "Intelligent and devout, yet given to rages and prone to episodic outbreaks of mental illness." Sounds like pretty much everyone in show business, nixing the devout part.

I am getting to a point with all of this. It's just hidden somewhere, like a Golden Ticket. Look, a bad plastic surgeon can really fuck up your life. Then again, it's really nice during awards season, as we call it out here in Los Angeles, to view an actress you haven't seen for a while and say to your significant other in bed, "She looks so much better this year, doesn't she?" and then they correct you: "That's 'cause the swelling went down, honey." (This comment pretty much includes everyone you could bash with exception of a true survivor, Mickey Rourke. When you look like that, you're entitled to walk around carrying your get-out-of-jail-free card.)

But back in the day, with no plastic surgery, all you could do was change your name. So Saget was originally something like Zaget, Zogut, Zagget. Interestingly enough, I did have an uncle named Bill *Sage*, not Saget. A great man. And such a nice name, Sage. Rolls off the tongue. Not like Saget. Add the *T* and you're in for it at school . . . Saget the Faggot, Sag-ass, Sag-nuts, Sag-balls— I've heard all the variables. As I got older I tried to make fun of my own name before other people did: "Sag-balls, don't mind if I do . . ."

Man, this is a cleansing, purging experience. And so is this book. It's fun to be able to release anything you want to say.

But back to names. I met the Zagat guy—of restaurant-guide fame—in an elevator in New York once. He didn't say a word until I broke the silence with something not so clever: "You're the Zagat guy, right? I've been told we are not related." Then after a minute or so of staring at me blankly with no emotion, he said, "No, we are definitely not related." I then asked if he could help me get restaurant reservations. Not my best move. He said, "No, I don't do that." He had a good presence though. Reminded me of the Community Chest guy in Monopoly, except no monocle. And much taller. And no mustache. Come to think of it, he was nothing like him.

I don't know what I'd have called myself if I could've picked my own name. If you could name yourself anything you wanted to, would you make your life easier and change your name to one word like Prince, Madonna, and Bono did? The great thing about life is you can change your name at any time. Maybe I'll release this book as Bob Mellencamp Saget. Or Jew-el. Or Bobby Gaga. Nah, I loved my dad so much I am proud to wear his last name, odd as it may be, like a banner. Displaying it completely nude across my chest with just the "Sash of Saget" creating a diagonal beauty pageant cover-up—from right nipple to left nut. This idea is so strong, I'm feeling a killer poster here to be sold at my concerts. It's all about the merch.

That's right, I'm proud to be the son of Ben and Dolly. My mother, Dolly, who is still around, is the matriarch of my family, being my mom and all. She is like a great snow owl in her late eighties . . . Love her. And everyone's kids and grandkids love her. That's my mama.

My early memories of Dolly are of her cooking family dinners for us when I was a kid. I wouldn't want to eat the food she prepared and my dad would reprimand me with, "Do you know what this meal would cost in a restaurant?" One time I answered him: "No, but I'd love to find out. Please can we go out to eat?"

I remember those family dinners as being loud and boisterous. There wasn't much room for conversation. There was a lot of love, but also a lot of fast talking and not much listening. Sounds like a lot of people's homes, right? I guess it's better than complete silence at the table. I've been over to people's homes where that's the case, and there's no easiness at a table of awkwardness. Woody

Allen broke the ice best in *Annie Hall* with his tension-defusing line: "Dynamite ham . . ."

If you're reading this book, perhaps you're of a similar demographic. Not necessarily Jewish, but let's say your upbringing was that of an "outsider." An observer. A survivor. Who grew up looking at their family, friends, the entire outside world, and wondering, What the fuck is wrong with me? Wait, is it me, or is it *them*? Odds are it's both.

In my life, and in my family, growing up could have been defined as "survival of the wittiest." I certainly wasn't the biggest jock. Because my dad was flattened out by his health issues during my childhood, he never played ball with me. I could kick ass at Keep Away and Red Rover, but that was about it.

Here's a pleasant flashback: Got into my first fistfight just at the end of sixth grade at Larrymore Elementary School in Norfolk. A kid who'd bullied me all year finally outdid himself with his anti-Semitic remarks, and so one day I accepted his offer of a "fair" fight on the baseball field behind the school. I wasn't exactly street-smart. Or cool. Or a fighter. Twenty kids gathered around to cheer us on. I was thrown because Buzzy, a guy who I'd thought was a friend of mine, rooted for that bastard I was fighting instead of me. After a bunch of bitch-slapping on my part, the shorter bully kicked me in the balls and my nose started to bleed profusely, which effectively ended the fight.

That night at home I asked my dad, "How come I got kicked in the balls and it was my nose that started to bleed?" He took his time to explain to me that "it's just one long connected muscle." I responded by asking him, "If that's the case, if I keep pushing on my nose, will my penis pop out more so I can be happier for the rest of my life?" My dad smiled. He basically raised me to believe I would grow from this experience, not my mojo, but my understanding of how to outthink your bully. "Young grasshopper, better to think ahead of kick-to-balls so nose does not bleed."

I didn't go to prom. I didn't have many friends. Throughout high school I didn't do drugs. Maybe that's why I didn't have many friends. But the few I had, I treasured. And you could count them on one hand, if you were missing a thumb. There were only a few of them—so I'm going to name them and give their cell numbers. *No.* No point in that. Who needs the lawsuits?

I did have a girlfriend at seventeen whom I ended up getting married to. And we had three amazing daughters. Then we got divorced. Please hold your applause till the end of this paragraph. Those statements are true. And I know them to be true because I Googled myself to write all this.

I also just looked myself up on Wikipedia and was relieved to see it no longer refers to my mom and dad, Dolly and Ben, as Minnie and Lenny. But it also says my "friends used to call me Sags." That isn't true. Dennis Miller started to call me Sags years after we'd first met when he was starting out in Cleveland and Pittsburgh. And once someone says on TV that that's your nickname, it becomes rote. I *wish* people had called me Sags growing up. I would've been way wannabe cooler with that nickname. But nope, for me it was Saget the Faggot. When guys called me that it hurt my feelings so much that to get back at them, I would blow them. No, I did not just type that, and no, you are not reading that in print. One-fourth of this book would have made my English teachers very proud.

I had one miraculous teacher who helped change the entire direction of my life. My senior English teacher in Abington, Pennsylvania, which is outside of Philly—her name was Elaine Zimmerman. A few years after she taught me, she was in a fatal car accident. I owe a lot to her. I was about to go to college, had enrolled in premed classes, and Mrs. Zimmerman literally told me, "Do not become a doctor. You need to make movies and perform and write. You need to make people laugh." I took her advice, changed my major at Temple University from pre-med to documentary filmmaking, and started performing as a stand-up comedian. I can only imagine, if I hadn't listened to her, how many patients I would've endangered. She saved thousands of lives.

And she was right. I needed to do something to make people laugh. Even in my youth. Although moving around so much was difficult, I was still a pretty carefree kid, showing off and getting silly-wild publicly whenever I could, even though lots of friends and relatives begged my parents to "ask Bobby to stop performing." I'd whip out the guitar, play up to forty serious songs I'd written, and then tell as many toilet-centered jokes as I could conjure up. The only good thing about it was fewer and fewer relatives came to visit because I'd scared them off.

My career in comedy was a direct result of being the kid in class who was screaming out for attention. Not like Sam Kinison yelling out—I was too well-mannered to scream out my frustrations. Sam was one of my favorites, though. We met in Houston and he was impossible not to take notice of. I helped tee up his first show-case at the Comedy Store and we were on *The 9th Annual HBO Young Comedians Special* together, along with Louie Anderson,

Bob Nelson, and Yakov Smirnoff. What a country. It was the first *Young Comedians Special* Rodney Dangerfield hosted.

People still ask me if I was a navy brat because I moved so much. I was born in Philadelphia, moved to Norfolk, Virginia, and lived there till I was fourteen, then moved to Encino, California, to learn about materialism, and then moved back to Philly at seventeen, just for my senior year, graduating from Abington. What you have just read is why I often got bad grades in English. I only had one teacher who gave extra credit for run-on sentences.

And as I've expounded on, I wasn't a navy brat, I was a meat brat. The son of a meathead. A brat-wurst. It wasn't easy relocating so much but I did okay. I ultimately got a girlfriend, but before that it was a struggle with the opposite sex. In ninth grade, when I lived in California, I wanted to take a girl to Disneyland. She was in tenth grade, a year older than me. I asked her if she'd like to go to "the Happiest Place on Earth." A statement like that is almost a lockdown for not getting laid. Upon my invite, she said, "No, thank you." It was also the first time I'd ever heard a girl say, "I like you as a friend." Hearing that repeatedly throughout your life can be like an emotional circumcision. That's a Rolling Stones song they left off their Chanukah album.

The Disneyland girl wasn't my first crush. My first was when I was five and on the short bus to kindergarten. I was crazy for three girls, Denise, Jodie, and Beth. My libido hadn't come in yet but I was semipopular because I was hyper and funny. Doesn't always serve me now. What I have in common today with my five-year-old self is that I believe dry-humping to be considered sex. Wait, it still is, isn't it?

Another big crush I had in prepuberty, besides every actress in a James Bond or Peter Sellers movie, was on my sixth-grade teacher in Norfolk, Mrs. Sherman. I was eleven. This kid named Buzzy was a guy I thought was my friend—but if you recall, he rooted for the bully in our big fight. Buzzy was more mature than any of us. He had pubes at nine. I had nine pubes at twelve.

Anyway, he had a crush on Mrs. Sherman as well, and to show his eleven-year-old love of her, he threw a pair of round-edged scissors at Mrs. Sherman's chest. They hit her in the bra and literally bounced off her boobs and sprang back into the classroom. I was immediately in love and inspired. Yes, I was twenty years younger than her, but she was sexy and smart and controlled me. Similar to my last relationship. Silly me, still in sixth grade emotionally. Till this book comes out—then I'm plowing through seventh.

But before I end this chapter, there is another older woman I want to pay homage to if I may, a matriarch in my family. My bubbe. I'm concerned that in print this could come off like I'm trying to name-drop Michael Bublé. I'm talking here about my bubbe—my grandmother. *Bubbe* is Yiddish and means "a huge fan of Michael Bublé."

I had two other wonderful grandparents too—my mother's father, Lou, and his wife, Bella Comer. They were just fine, and I loved them and all that, but no one had the cute charisma of my dad's mom, my bubbe.

Bubbe is pronounced "bubbee," a befitting name for a woman who was short, prideful, smart, selfless, and a bit bubbly. She was born in Russia and was sent here by my grandfather once he paved the way to bring his family over to Philadelphia. My bubbe's accent was a meld of Russian, Yiddish, English, and whatever language came from a town called Varclan, which doesn't exist anymore. Too hard to spell, so the Cossacks leveled it.

My bubbe was well aware she did not excel at languages. But the sound of her name brought all the grandchildren joy. It wasn't just from hearing the funny sound of the word *bubbe*. Her husband was dying of liver cancer. Don't think he dealt too well with trying to run a tailor shop and having five sons and a daughter. And yes, those same five sons and daughter were my father and his siblings—and the boys, who, unbeknownst to themselves, continually were becoming inducted into the Heart Attack Club.

One nice story I recall about my bubbe: She was visiting my parents and me when I was fourteen. At that time we were living in the San Fernando Valley, as my dad had just transferred to California from Virginia. It was the only way he could keep his job with the food company. He had a lot of pride in his work, and my bubbe, his mother, was prideful too. Never wanted anyone to see her at night after all her "gear" came off. Before she went to bed she took off her girdle, removed her two hearing aids, put up her small amount of hair in an industrial-strength net, and dropped her teeth in a glass of Efferdent.

I played tricks on her relentlessly. I was an asshole. I didn't have any friends, so I chose my grandmother to be the object of all my hazing. She'd have to go to the bathroom and I wouldn't let her go. She'd yell, "Bobby, I have to take off my girdle, let me go! I'm gonna make it in my pants!" And I'd laugh and say, "But, Bubbe, I love you so much, I'll miss you, please don't leave me!" I am ashamed to say I was a teenage dickweed. No different from the idiot boys who tweet me now and say dumb shit just to mess with people. It ended well—she never soiled herself and we always laughed about my behavior over the dinner table: "Listen to what Bobby did to me today . . ." Each day she visited had become a comedic adventure.

Anyway, there's a payoff to this particular story. On February 9, 1971, at six A.M., my whole family was jolted awake by an earthquake. It was a huge quake and didn't seem like it was going to stop. I ran into my bubbe's room and her bed was literally moving back and forth. The closets were swinging open and closed. She sat up, furious with me, and yelled, "Bobby, stop shaking my bed!" It was a bad-silent-film moment where I was trying to explain what was happening as she was grabbing her hearing aids. I left her and staggered to my parents' room. I remember them getting dressed and then taking me in their arms, bringing me under one of the doorway arches made of drywall and a brittle wood frame, to kiss me good-bye in case the world was ending.

It was the famous Sylmar quake we'd experienced. Looking out the windows you could see the sidewalk rolling like gentle ocean waves. It lasted about a minute and at the time, I recall, they measured it as having a magnitude of 7.1. Since then, history, and I guess the devices they measure quakes with, reassessed it as a 6.6. Like everything else in life, with time it got marked down. Shoulda sold it when it got to 6.8. I used to have a joke that came from that experience. I had a nightmare I was getting a vasectomy and there was an earthquake during the surgery. The doctor came in to tell me the bad news: "Sorry, Bob, it was a 7.1 but now it's a 6.4." I'd always look all proud at the setup. "That's right, it was a 7.1."

Losing my bubbe was tough for me. Tough for all of us: my cousins, my aunt, my sisters, my parents. She was in a convalescent home in Philadelphia and I would sit at her bedside singing love songs I'd written for her. She rallied and seemed to recover from the severe stroke she'd had, but by the time I played a third original song for her, she knew that it was time to go.

In sci-fi horror movies we often discover, right as the world is about to be wiped out, that something as simple as fire or water can destroy the invaders from another galaxy. For my poor bubbe, fire and water would have been a reprieve. There is nothing more dangerous for a person on the razor's edge of life than the shrill falsetto tones of a sixteen-year-old boy belting out love songs before his voice has changed.

She was one of the greatest women of my life. And I don't think my singing had anything to do with her demise. Others have not been so lucky. I was playing "You Are My Sunshine" once in my backyard and on the lyric "You'll never know, dear, how much I love you," a squirrel had a heart attack in midair and plummeted to its death. Nature doesn't lie.

Chapter 3

THE LOSS OF TWO GREAT WOMEN

This chapter is about two women who meant the world to me. No, it is not about a three-way with two waitresses—that story comes later. In fact, I have to make it up. Look, there's no easy way to segue into this; what I'm about to describe is some painful stuff. Life's interesting. Sometimes it just sucks. Sometimes your heart gets broken. My heart's been broken several times, and not that long ago. It may be broken again by the time this book goes to paperback, and again for the audiobook.

I'm not telling you anything that's not the obvious. We all go through pain and heartache. It's part of the journey. Just when we think we're on the upswing and have achieved some kind of breakthrough or closure, something else hits. It's like the family I once heard about who left California because they were scared of earthquakes and moved to Colorado, where a massive boulder fell on their house. That sonofabitch coyote.

Our destiny is not usually what we expect it to be. I've known lots of people who've tried to plan exactly how things would turn out for them, and then when life didn't go according to plan, they ended up in denial. They just couldn't accept that their end point was different than what they'd envisioned. Acceptance of endings has been pretty difficult for me too. It's painful for me right now just to end this paragraph.

There's a great quote about the difficulty of "endings" that comes directly from movie star and occasional hero Tom Cruise. He said, "Nothing ends nicely, that's why it ends." That's true of a relationship for sure, but the quote could also apply to the end of a life. That's right, I'm using a Tom Cruise quote to introduce my personal stories of loss.

You always have to be careful to choose the *right* Tom Cruise quote. If you're looking at your father in a coffin and up comes your uncle, Ralph Kramden–style, yelling into the casket, *"SHOW ME THE MONEY, BABY!!!"* I'd say that's not the appropriate quote for the moment. Maybe that's where the expression *cry uncle* came from.

I looked up the roots of the expression *cry uncle* and it involves being tickled by a friend to the point of begging for help—from your uncle. It also refers back to ancient Roman days when young boys would yell out in Latin, *"Patrue mi patruissime,"* which, translated, means, "Please tell your uncle to take his finger out of my butthole." I'm not sure if that's the exact translation, but wherever it came from, it too did not end well.

So the Cruise quote was, "Nothing ends nicely . . ." Sometimes a person's life does in fact end relatively nicely—compared to how it could've ended. Especially if there's suffering involved. And for people you care deeply about, the less suffering they have to go through, the better.

Having lost quite a few people over the years, I know that when someone dies or is dying, you just want to ease their pain, even end it if you can. That's why euthanasia can be simpler than divorce. Oh wait, I didn't type that. But wait, you read it, so I must have. Silly me. Or maybe if you read like I do, you just skimmed, and so it didn't register and I'm safe.

I've been talking a lot with my friends lately about death and divorce. I've been obsessed with these subjects for years actually. Sometimes it seems like death, the finality of it, is easier to go through than a breakup. I wouldn't imagine most people share that opinion, yet I've found when I bring it up among friends they understand exactly what I'm talking about. Or seem to, until they storm out of the dinner party crying.

It's not an easy subject, death. It's up there with politics and religion, in that it tends to lead to some pretty heated discussion. If, say, you are dating someone, and you have plans to possibly have sex with them, do not bring up death. Unless the person you're dating is an undertaker, in which case you just found your way in.

Inevitably, going back through our lives and remembering people we've lost makes us think of our own mortality. When I was a teenager, having a different uncle die every couple years, I never pictured myself making it past my fifties. Then, losing my two sisters so young, I felt even more like a sword of Damocles was hanging over my head. When was it going to be my turn?

I don't feel that way anymore. Maybe I shouldn't jinx it by putting that in print. But these days I see myself in the future and I try to envision a kind, horny old man walking around making people laugh whenever I can. In front of the camera, behind the camera, inserting the camera into myself, then having surgery to have it removed . . . Strange to imagine one's own death. When I imagine it now, I see it as a sort of dramatic spontaneous combustion. Like I'll just be walking down the street and from the sheer overamped energy I've gone through my entire life with, I'll blow up. Just disintegrate. But cleanly. I won't want anyone walking by me covered by my remains of the day.

All of this death talk is leading toward the subject of this chapter, which is my two sisters, who were taken from us too soon. I feel a bit narcissistic discussing my personal losses, knowing so many people reading this have suffered their own. But this is my book, so here goes.

I lost two of the most important women in my life. They were my two older sisters. Andi (short for Andrea) died at age thirty-four of a brain aneurysm. And then years later, Gay lost her life at the age of forty-seven to the disease scleroderma. In the years since, I've been very active as a board member of the Scleroderma Research Foundation, trying to raise money to fund the research to help find a cure for this rare disease.

I feel badly I haven't done as much in the name of my sister Andi to fund brain aneurysm research. And I've only done a few benefits for the American Heart Association, even though heart disease is a cause I should pay closer attention to, since all of my uncles and my dad had heart attacks. It's just part of who I am that I try to raise money for people who are suffering. And having a benefit seems the easiest way to make money quickly if you're part of a non-profit charity not funded by the NIH. My phone died recently and I held a benefit for it. Sure is quiet in here.

I loved my sisters, Andi and Gay, very much. They were six and ten years older than me, respectively. They were both school-teachers. Really good ones. Which means they were underpaid and loved to impart as much wisdom and goodness as they could to their students. I still meet people today who tell me how much Andi and Gay changed their lives.

Honestly I don't know how my parents did it. They lost four children in total—twins before I was born and then my sisters. My mom tells me, "Not a day goes by that I don't think of them." She's not speaking only of grief and sadness either. That's one of the things I love most about my mom. She speaks of her deceased children the way brave mothers and fathers I've met throughout my life often speak of children they have lost, no matter what the circumstance. They learn, as much as they can, not to dwell on the sadness and instead remember the good times and focus on them.

When tragedy strikes, it's more important than ever to look for anything that can bring humor and joy to every moment. When my sister Gay was in the hospital, we joked about how bad the food was—two slices of bologna on white bread with mayo. So I broke hospital rules and went to Jerry's Deli and got her chicken matzo ball soup and a turkey sandwich. In her sick state she could barely eat it, but it was definitely better food. In retrospect, I probably shouldn't have snuck in that stuffed cabbage. Even she laughed when her gas got so bad that one of her farts knocked a Dixie cup off her dinner tray. Some people say it was coincidence but I believe it was a force bigger than any of us in that room— cabbage gas.

Not only that, but she died so long ago, at Cedars-Sinai Medical Center in Los Angeles, the Jerry's Deli across the street where I got the chicken soup is now closed. It's one thing to take my sister from me, but, Lord God, why did you have to close a deli that made a decent Reuben and had good potato salad?

Comic relief truly comes at the strangest moments. I had so many laughs with my father during his hospice time. Laughter through tears hits more senses than most human experience. When you're laughing and crying simultaneously, the tears often run down your cheeks and roll into your open mouth. It's shocking how salty tears are when you're not used to tasting them. And if you *are* used to tasting tears, well, that's a compelling fetish you have, my friend. And one that requires real skill—to be able to cry on cue, then tilt your head back so you can drink your teardrops . . . or do you just get off on making someone else cry and then licking their tears? That's just creepy.

What's creepier is there exists out there in the world a certain percentage of people reading this who can relate—and also get off on licking tears. I don't want to know them. Creepy weird tear lickers. Yet, I am not here to judge.

I remember when I was in my teens and my family had just gone through my uncles' deaths, we were sitting around the dinner table feeling emotional. This was also soon after my dad's heart attack, and my mom had stopped cooking with salt, because the doctor had told him to steer clear of sodium. I remember my sister Andi started to cry at the table and I made a comment to the effect of: "Good thing we're all crying—our tears dripping onto this dry chicken is the only shot we have to add any taste to it!" Silly, old-school, and not particularly clever, but an icebreaker nonetheless, one that made us all laugh and feel better. The kind of dumb humor I got from my dad, adding levity where there wasn't any called for. But there was a solace in it.

My sister Gay is not someone who would have cried at the table. She was pretty different from Andi—stoic, but with an underlying strength and intelligence. What she went through health-wise changed the lives of everyone in our family forever. It definitely changed her life, because it took it. For me, it made me angry at first, to see her suffer. When you can't do anything to help someone you love, you go through all the stages.

Eventually, her illness made me a champion for a disease that strangely enough I had fortuitously become involved with years before she was diagnosed with it. In 1984 I was cold-called by this great lady, Sharon Monsky, the founder of the Scleroderma Research Foundation. She asked me to perform at a benefit with other comedians to help raise money for research. A year earlier, Robin Williams had been the first comedian to ever perform to help the Foundation. I did the benefit a few months later.

At that time, my sister Gay was completely healthy, apart from some asthma that had been with her since childhood—definitely no signs of an autoimmune or vascular disease. But a couple years later, when I performed again at the same benefit, Gay had finally been diagnosed (after many disturbing misdiagnoses) with scleroderma.

Scleroderma is a rare disease that often affects women in the prime of their lives. When I hosted the benefit once more a year later, my sister Gay was actually in the audience and at this point she was deteriorating fast. It was tragic. Then, a year later, at another Foundation event, I announced that Gay had lost her battle with the disease. Since then, I have been involved in every benefit, and in the past ten years I have been a proud member of the SRF, which has raised over thirty million dollars to help fund research supporting those affected by this disease that took my sister.

All right, I know you paid good money to read this book, and now, all of a sudden, I've gone to this sorrowful I-lost-my-sisters place, sans humor, with a plug for my cause. Apologies. Shit happens. I think Confucius said that. I believe he also said, "Man who help others with an open heart will be thanked tenfold with much hot pussy." Again, just wanted to see if you were still reading or just skimming this chapter.

Thanks for bearing with me. Look, they asked if I wanted to write a book and I said, "Sure, I love writing." Just didn't know how I would pinch this one out. But I'm glad I did. Everyone should write a book. Or at least a pamphlet. Or a PDF. Or a mimeo. I miss mimeos. There's so little these days for kids to get high from in school. Oh yeah, except for booze and drugs.

But getting back to my sisters, when Andi was thirty-four she gave me a book on past lives, *Seth Speaks: The Eternal Validity of the Soul* by Jane Roberts and Robert F. Butts. I was immediately drawn in because I misread the title and thought it was about butts. I soon realized it was about something completely different, about reincarnation and how the soul lives on forever. The book set me on a path of discovery that went on for the next ten years. Not more than two weeks after my sister gave me that book, out of nowhere she had a brain aneurysm and passed away. Again, please hold your laughter until the end of the book. It was not a funny time.

I vividly remember getting the call from my mother. I was in Detroit at a club called the Comedy Castle, working for a friend, Mark Ridley, the club owner. You find out who your true friends are when they console you through the hard times. Mark was amazing. And he was a club owner. You can count the number of kind club owners on your penis. That's not completely true. In my earlier years as a comedian I did become friends with a couple other club owners. However, I can't print their names here because they are all in prison.

So it was a Saturday night in Detroit and it was a very dark moment. My mom called and said, "Hello, Bob?"

"Yes."

"It's Andi, Bob."

There was a long pause and I said nothing.

"She's dead, Bob."

All I recall through the emotion and shock was the gesture of pounding my fist into the air and saying quietly to myself, "You go, Andi—you evolve and go to where you want to go, to be at peace." She had suffered a lot in her short life. The sweetest, most emotional girl you could ever meet.

Randy Newman wrote a song, "Real Emotional Girl," that I think describes Andi perfectly. I was in an acting class in my early twenties with my teacher Darryl Hickman, and I sang the song as a monologue/exercise. It's a real heartbreaker. It goes: "She's a real emotional girl / She wears her heart on her sleeve / Every little thing you tell her / She'll believe / She really will . . ."

That was Andi. She was vulnerable, kind, and easily influenced. A bit lost. Like the girl in the song: "She even cries in her sleep / I've heard her / Many times before / I never had a girl who loved me / Half as much as this girl loves me / She's real emotional."

I will always miss Andi; she is forever in my heart. I wish I could've done something to help her live a full life, or even just a better life than she had before we lost her at thirty-four.

With her sudden death came a flood of emotion for our whole family. But we all shared the knowledge that she was no longer in pain. For any parent, the loss of a child is the worst thing you can go through. Although being disemboweled in the town square is a close second. Mel Gibson was never as likable as when they cut his guts out in *Braveheart*.

I've always had a fascination with death, being surrounded by so much of it growing up. At that time in my life, I believed it was therapeutic to think about what happens when we die. Some feel our soul goes on to another incarnation and that it keeps growing and learning. I just don't want to ever go to a place where there are no deli meats. Honestly, I'm not sure what happens when we get out of here, but I do know I'm a lover of human life. I believe that people are basically good and pure at heart. Especially if they're holding a chicken salad sandwich. How can you not trust someone holding a chicken salad sandwich?

Allow me please to make my earlier point clearer. I believe *most* people are good and pure at heart. I try to see the good in everyone, I really do. Even when I'm on a long, nightmarish plane flight and looking around in horror at my fellow passengers . . . at the couple arguing at the top of their lungs so everyone can hear . . . at the guy next to me whom I made the mistake of saying hello to, which led to a six-hour monologue detailing every aspect of his life, from his ex-wives drama to his bowel obstructions . . . at the lady behind me sneezing violently, not covering her face, just unleashing hot snot into the air, most of it directed all over me . . .

When I'm in that situation, I look at all these people and I try to visualize what's beautiful about them. I may have to work a little harder, and I may have a tough time pushing out all the negative thoughts about these strangers invading my personal space. I may start to have an existential crisis, but then I breathe and try to imagine what their stories are. I say to myself, Bob, you're just frustrated being around all these people in this hot, cramped aircraft and it's making you focus on their worst qualities—but people are still basically good. I know in my soul that people are basically good.

I look across at the young mother and her baby sitting on the other side of me—a baby who could grow up to do something wonderful like find the cure for cancer. What could be more pure and good than a little baby who grows up to find the cure for cancer? I look at the guy with the ex-wife drama and feel better about him—he's now sleeping peacefully, thanks to a couple Ambien. He's not so bad, I think.

But then, it happens: The pilot announces, "We're starting our descent." And no one puts their seat upright or stops their way-too-loud conversation, and the baby suddenly throws up and some of it hits me. Yet, even then, I keep it together, thinking to myself, these people may not appear to be the best at this moment, but they are basically good people. And we all deserve to get to Ohio. Let's do this.

And then the man next to me on sleeping pills sharts his pants. Loud and wet.

People are only human. I do treasure life. I want that little up-chucking baby to grow up healthy and happy. Maybe he won't find a cure for cancer, but who knows, maybe he'll run a big company and earn a lot of money that will at least go toward the good of supporting his family—until he gets caught embezzling and cheating on his wife and is sentenced for white-collar crime. Then again, maybe he'll turn out like the guy who just sharted his pants. We are all still only human. If you're not alive, and you are a soul floating around in the ether somewhere, you do not get the privilege of sharting your pants. That's right, I'm saying it is a privilege to shart your pants. To butt-queef. Because butt-queefing means you are alive. I don't know, but my guess is when you're dead, you can't hear loud sounds like a fart or smell bad scents like poo. Or the cougars or possible hookers who come in groups late at night in swanky hotel restaurants reeking of Febreze. Life is a gift.

Back to this whole philosophical, questioning thing I've been jagging on: Are people basically good? What are we here for? What happens after we die? All this questioning is a direct result of the emotional scars of my younger years, particularly the loss of my two sisters. It's not so much a religious thing. I'd like to believe my sisters are in a better place now. But I do understand why some say there is nothing after this life and when you die you are dead and gone.

I spoke to a friend of mine recently who flat-out told me, "There is no God, Bob. Period. No God, no ghosts, no nothin'." I know quite a few people who are positive that when you die you just "cut to black," like Tony Soprano in the last episode of *The Sopranos*. Which sadly brings up memories of James Gandolfini, who also was taken from us much too soon.

But personally, I can't shake the feeling that there's more to it than just cutting to black. Maybe this has something to do with the family story I'm going to tell now, a story that might be a little chilling to readers, especially if you're into numerology or astrology. And who isn't? Awkward pause. C'mon, the zodiac is in our newspapers every day. Okay, not in the *New York Times* or *Wall Street Journal*, but I can always rely on the *Los Angeles Times* for my Taurus emotional temperature.

Here's the story . . . Two years before I was born, my mom had given birth to full-term healthy twins. And when I say two years before I was born, I mean two years to the *day:* May 17, 1954. I was born on May 17, 1956. The twins who were born two years earlier were named Robert and Faith. Like I said, they were both born healthy, but the hospital in Philly had recently been infested with dysentery and no one told any of the parents who had given birth that week. I don't know exactly what happened but as my mother conveys it now, about seven babies died along with the twins. Robert and Faith lived only seven and eight days, respectively.

Then, two years *to the day* that they were born, I was born—is that an astrologer's wet dream or what? So that seeming coincidence always stuck with me, and because of it I was very receptive when my sister Andi gave me the book about the soul's journey through different incarnations. It made sense to me at that time, as if it was all some kind of cosmic do-over. Heartbreaking, and yet I was honored my mom and dad had bestowed the name Robert on me.

To this day, I feel blessed to have been named Robert. Why they named my sister Gay, I don't know. When she was born in 1946, *gay* only meant "happy." The joke we have all heard is "And it still does, baby!!" But with the last name Saget, my sister had it doubly rough as she got older. People can be cruel, even if they are basically good. The fact that our family's last name rhymes with *faggot* is obvious and sophomoric, but ironically those are two personality traits necessary to be a bully and a name-caller. Gay was a great teacher, but if a student didn't like her, they would call her "Gay Faggot," which is not only hurtful, but even more in present times, once again, redundant.

Both of my sisters were amazing people and I will always miss them. Until I see them again. *If* that's how it works. But what my family went through—all the tragedy and all the pain, both before and after I was born—is what created and fostered that crucial comedy/survival gene, which revealed itself most markedly in my father and in me. It was this part of my DNA that allowed me to lose two of the most important people in my life and push even harder to pursue a career in making people laugh.

Chapter 4

SURVIVING STAND-UP

Sometimes I can't believe what I went through to become a comedian. What I subjected myself to: ten years of open mics, doing anything to get stage time . . . and still, I never slept with anyone to get a gig. Who could sleep while you were being mounted by a club owner from behind? Like a lot of beginners in comedy, I was coming from a young insecure place of wanting people to like me. I lived like most actors and comedians live when they're just "a kid with a dream": in a single apartment in a part of L.A. with the occasional sound of late-night gunfire.

The kid-with-a-dream thing is a cliché but it's true. In order to have a chance of making it in any kind of career in the arts, you have to start with full-blown idealism and a belief that you'll succeed even though everyone tells you, "It's impossible, you won't make it." The people who say that are, in some cases, just not right.

But on the flip side, if you are incorrect about your super-talent, there may be a field you're better suited for . . . a cool Internet company, welding, fluffer . . . Show business is hard as fuck, so if you're perhaps a young person who's thinking about getting into it but you're undecided, I'd recommend you jump at any opportunity you have to avoid the pain of it. But if you know this is what you want and you're driven beyond belief, then go for it. Carpe diem.

Some young people ask me for career advice. I know . . . me. And then I try to answer them with something valuable. It's complicated because some people just want to be a *star* to show up everyone in their life who thought they'd never amount to anything. That mind-set makes me throw up in my mouth a little. It's tough to give advice to a person who has only that as their motivation—rather than any desire to cultivate a talent. I understand it. Sometimes it's youth. Sometimes it's delusion. I suffered from both. These days I love the craft of it all—writing, stand-up, acting, directing, producing, and dancing to "Gangnam Style" in a onesie with Velcro eyeholes.

You can't listen to what other people think about you or your work. You've got to just follow your instincts. Most people don't know shit. That's not true, most people do know shit. And shit stinks. Although I once knew a woman whose shit really didn't stink. That's what she thought, and she was right. Because it just didn't. I won't say her name, but here's a picture of her. No, I wouldn't. Not in this chapter.

Back online: So you can't let anyone define you. In my career, if I had let other people define me, I could've ended up dustbusting the halls of a YMCA and asking the other tenants if they wanted to buy some bootlegged tapes of people getting hit in the nuts.

The balance for me was to suppress my renegade "id" and stay open and learn from other people whom I was enlightened by being around. I was influenced by many individuals, some famous, some not. My biggest inspirations as a young stand-up were the comedians I would watch every chance I got, sitting in the back of the Comedy Store or the Improv late at night: Richard Pryor, David Letterman, Billy Crystal, Robin Williams, Andy Kaufman, Michael Keaton . . . to name six. The list of people I learned from was endless. Still is. To this day, I'll drop by a club late at night to meet a stand-up friend and stare at the stage in awe watching a super-talented new guy or girl who just "has something." And some of the time it's on their lip.

In the early eighties I also learned from people who were less known—comedians who remain undiscovered today, who are only appreciated by true "comedyphiles" and by those who knew them back when. There are some comics who were and still are gut funny—who everyone thought were going to "pop" as the newest comedy stars but for some reason didn't. They took chances on-stage and for whatever reason, their path didn't get to be realized in the way it deserved. Many were self-destructive and some just had a bout of bad luck. They say luck is when opportunity and preparedness meet. They also say, "Your lucky numbers are 2, 7, 13, 44 . . . 66 . . ." Jeff Ross. Just felt like writing his name here. He's a buddy of mine. He loves Chinese food, yoga, and changing his hairstyle as often as he changes his underwear. Once a month.

Comedians are obsessed with their bodies, no matter what shape they are in. I knew several comedians over the years who would come out onstage completely nude. Maybe they did it for shock value or just to show they didn't give a shit. Going onstage nude is a public act that can work for or against you. I am certain it would work against me.

A guy named Ollie Joe Prater did it once. Ollie was a likable, rotund, Yosemite Sam–type guy who wanted to take the stage once while Richard Pryor and Robin Williams were on simultaneously in the Main Room of the Comedy Store. The only way to upstage the two of them was to come out with his cowboy hat and boots on—and nothing else. It worked on some level. I mean, I'm mentioning it in this book, so it stayed with me.

But I wasn't sure exactly how it happened so I called my friend director/writer Mike Binder to get my facts straight. His response was calming for me: "I remember it as if it were yesterday. It sure did happen. I was there." I asked Mike, "So Ollie came out naked except for cowboy boots and a hat completely nude and stood between Robin and Pryor on the Main Room stage?" Mike responded, "Yep. With his dick tucked in between his legs to make it look like a vagina." So it is written, and so it was done.

Another comedian I'd come up with at the time who came out nude was the brilliant Jim Carrey. Jim's reason was much simpler. A bunch of us had performed on the Comedy Store's twentieth-anniversary special and during the curtain call Jim came out naked and stood right next to me with just a sock over his dick. Part of my instinct was to pull it off, and the other part was to move away.

What I remember most is wondering if he'd attached double-stick tape to it, or was his penis just that wide. The man to this day has a genius's balls. In retrospect, they must have been shoved into the sock along with his dick. In any case, it was funny and memorable, and as soon as tape stopped rolling, I ran away. I could've run away the moment he did it, but then I guess I thought I'd have looked like I had a televised moment of gay panic, so I waited until they were done filming. So I could have a moment of gay panic not on tape. Another conundrum had presented itself. It's hard to upstage a naked person. Then again, if you've ever watched a porn film, your eyes will sometimes focus on the only person who's dressed.

Starting out in stand-up requires a vivid imagination. You need one to actually go up onstage and think you have something to share that people would even want to hear and could find compelling and amusing. And you have to be in the zone to perform whatever that is and enjoy being there. Lots of things have to align for standup to just *happen*.

For me it took ten years to even start to happen. All I knew was, I wanted to go onstage and entertain the people as much as I could—either with what I had prepared or with something I made up spontaneously on the spot. All of my early humor sprang from some kind of warped truism. Sick jokes, all about my girlfriend, my parents, my youth, career self-deprecation—the usual topics for a beginning comic.

One of my first jokes was "My mother never let me go to camp as a little kid because she thought I'd get embarrassed undressing in front of little boys. But I kind of like it now . . . That's not true, I like it a lot . . . That's not true, I'm not a senator."

That was the closest I came to political satire at the time. I don't recall what senator was in trouble for being a pedophile. But the camp part was true. My mom was overly strict with me, partly because camp cost money that we didn't have a ton of. So instead of going to camp, I stayed home and mowed lawns every summer, which also has lascivious connotations. So as absurd as my beginnings as a stand-up were, there was always truth at the root, which was an interesting thing to come to grips with, because throughout my childhood I was pretty much a serial liar.

I had been perjuring myself since I was about nine, because I didn't want to get in trouble with my mom and other authority figures. My dad was always busy working and having weekly heart attacks, so my mom was the taskmaster at home. Again, authoritative mothers are often textbook stuff if you're going to wind up in comedy. And textbook stuff if you're a human being. Repression leads to rebellion. Took me thirty years to not be able to lie anymore. A'ight, forty years. Do I hear fifty?

We have all lied. Because we don't want to disappoint. Animals lie. They learn it from us. Ask your cat if they're the one who crapped on the carpet and they'll try to distract you to take your mind off the fact that their cat turd is sitting in the middle of the living room. But who hasn't done that? "Bob, did you shit in the living room?" "No, Dad, it must've been Mom."

My dad would always laugh at stuff like that. He was my biggest comedy influence. He turned me on to Jack Benny, Burns and Allen, all the old radio comedians. He was also a huge fan of his own childhood heroes, the silent film comedians like Harold Lloyd. My dad liked Lloyd better than Chaplin. I would disagree with him on that. At nine years old. The only thing worse than a nine-year-old who thinks he knows everything is . . . Well, there are a lot of things worse, but a nine-year-old who thinks he knows everything is pretty fucking annoying.

I was influenced by just about anyone who was inspired and passionate about what they did, which turned out for me to be mostly filmmakers and comedians. My path as a kid was laid way before I was.

When I was about eleven, I used to send away to Blackhawk Films in Davenport, Iowa, and buy all the eight-millimeter silent films of Chaplin, Lloyd, and others. Just loved movies—didn't matter there was no sound, I would sit and watch them with subtitles. I loved Groucho and took in every comedian I could on television. Not a lot of edginess to be had in the early sixties. Quickness of wit was the edginess of the time. The spontaneous performances of TV icons like Jack Paar, Ernie Kovacs, Steve Allen, Johnny Carson, Dean Martin. Those guys were quick-witted and classy, professional.

I also loved the same things everybody loved: Lucy, Jackie Gleason, and anything I could pick up from what I was too young to have seen when it was the number one show on television: *Your Show of Shows*. Later, I was obsessed with *The Dick Van Dyke Show*. And *Get Smart*. And then anything made separately or together by Carl Reiner and Mel Brooks.

Comedy is a highly subjective art form. There are those who would possibly prefer *my* comedy if it had come out during silent film days—*mit* out sound, a term coined by a 1920s German-émigré director. If only I'd been born German and silent. With the personality I have, if I was born in Germany in the twenties, I would have been silenced for sure.

I never got to see heroes like Chaplin in the flesh, but amazingly when I was fourteen, Larry Fine of the Three Stooges spoke at my middle school, Mulholland Junior High. This was during the time my family was living in L.A., having moved from Norfolk for my dad's job as head of meat. I was only at that school for six months, but the Larry experience stuck with me my whole life. He was already quite old at that point and not in great health, but I was starstruck.

I adored the Three Stooges and was so enamored with Larry that I asked him after the assembly if I could visit him at the

Motion Picture and Television Country House and Hospital, in Woodland Hills, where he lived—supported thankfully by the Screen Actors Guild. He said, "Sure," although it was hard to understand him as he'd had a pretty bad stroke a couple years earlier. I think his actual response was more like "Schlllhompmpmphhh."

I was dying to talk to him more, hear all about his life, and pump him for more great Stooges stories. Not pump him sexually; I'm sure some of your minds went to that place. Remember, I was only fourteen and puberty didn't come for me until I'd gotten my learner's permit. Anyway, long story short—you're welcome—my mother, Dolly, drove me to visit Larry at the Motion Picture residence. He was very happy to have a guest.

The first time I went, he told me how tough his life was inside the nursing home. He never got to see any of the old shorts he'd made with Moe and Curly—and Shemp and Curly Joe—because the place didn't have UHF. There was no cable, and back then they only ran Three Stooges shorts on UHF channels.

Until I wrote these words, I hadn't even thought of the acronym *UHF* for decades. It's crazy; this writing and reminiscing is the only thing that makes me feel older. That, and my knees and my back and fupa, which fluctuates in size weekly.

In that first visit with Larry, he also told me about how much he'd gotten hurt in the Stooges films. How Moe Howard would have them do their own stunts and they'd fall and break ribs. And how sometimes when Moe would rip out pieces of Larry's hair in a slapstick fashion on camera, real hair would come out with it. Hair extensions are not always a friend of comedy.

I'll never forget that before we said good-bye that day, I went with Larry to go pick up his new set of false teeth at the front desk. With his good leg he kicked himself straight backward in his wheelchair—he couldn't wheel himself forward because one side of his body was inactive, so he'd have spun around in circles if he'd tried. When we finally got to the reception desk, he picked up the envelope from the receptionist, ripped it open without missing a beat, and popped his new set of falsies right into his mouth.

I'm glad he didn't wash them off first. I didn't want our visit interrupted by any kind of hygiene. It felt exactly like a Three Stooges moment. Bittersweet. Funny and sad. They often go hand in hand, especially with comedy people from a different era.

My next visit to Larry, I brought along the silent eight-millimeter Stooges shorts from Blackhawk Films that I'd bought with money I'd made as a retail clerk. At that time I was working in a store in Reseda, a job my dad had teed up for me, and actually it was in that same store that I had my own Three Stooges–like moment . . .

I was pricing Corelle dinner plates late one night when some armed men burst in, ran through to the sporting goods section to steal shotguns and bullets—yes, they sold those in a Target-like store in L.A. back then—and proceeded to fire off rounds as they grabbed cash and hauled ass through the aisles to make a getaway. I ducked behind the dinnerware display, because I knew those items were made by Corning (my mom had them) and they didn't break when you dropped them, so I figured they could stop a bullet. Luckily, no shots were fired in my direction, but I still hid behind dinner plates, the fifteen-year-old pussy that I was.

So by the time I had turned fifteen, all I cared about was comedy and old films. Oh yeah, and smuggled *Playboys*. When my mom drove me to see Larry—with my projector and *mit*-out-sound Stooges shorts in tow—I couldn't wait to show him the old reels. Three Stooges shorts were an acquired taste for some. For a fifteen-year-old boy, they were the shit. But without sound, there were no sound effects, no Moe going, "C'mere, you," and ripping out Larry's hair, no *"Boink!"* when he poked Curly in the eyes. No "Whoop-whoop-whoop-whoop-whoop" from Curly.

Larry seeing himself in those films touched him deeply. He told me he hadn't seen them in ten years. I found that hard to believe, but it was true. He told me his producer, Jules White, had taken all the money and left him with nothing. Later I'd hear the same story time and time again from various comedy icons about their own lots in life. By the end of our visit, Larry was crying and so was I.

What he and the other Stooges went through is what paved the way for many who came after—working for the man, getting the laughs and maybe some fame but not being rewarded for it. They were legends to me, even though some to this day consider them lowbrow. I visited Larry a few more times but then I decided to stop. I wasn't related to him, it's creepy to be a young fan, and I didn't want to bring him down any more. I felt bad that all he wanted to tell me about were the hardships he'd been through his whole life.

It might seem strange that even though I worshipped the Three Stooges and was a budding student of comedy, I had no idea at this early age that I would end up with a career in show business. I'd always planned on becoming a doctor. At that time, it was just part of who I was. I was a lover of comedy, films, and apparently, old men who'd had strokes.

I spent the next few years a little lost, trying to figure out where I fit in. Had no clue what I wanted to do. For the sake of moving this story forward, let's just say the ages of fifteen to seventeen were not much fun. I was overweight, with zits, and my signature look at the time was a late-seventies comb-over and welding-size bling-y PhotoGray glasses. Bling.

Shocking as it may be, even donning my welding glasses and possessing my über-nerd eight-millimeter film collection, I was not considered cool. I made a few good friends of value, and I'm fortunate to still keep in touch with some of them. I did some way-below-par student films—*Hitler on the Roof* with Neil Leiberman and Bob Kohn in L.A., and in Philly, *Beach Blanket Blintzes,* with my dear friend Gary Wagner, about a giant Claymation blintz who got on top of the Empire State Building and turned people into sour cream. It was much worse than it sounds.

It was after eleventh grade that I moved from L.A. to Philly, where I graduated from Abington Senior High. My dad helped me get a job in a supermarket deli. I used to have nightmares of slicing my face down in layers on the deli slicer, reminiscent of an M. C. Escher painting.

It was also around this time that I started to think about comedy as something I might actually get paid for someday. I had always gotten off on making people laugh, in my household and at school. I still didn't think I'd actually become a stand-up, but somehow it just started to happen.

At about seventeen, on a fluke, I entered an FM radio station contest (WMMR in Philadelphia) and won. I went onstage at a club and sang a song I'd written called "Bondage." At seventeen. I wasn't exactly Janis Ian, although I looked like her a little. I'm glad the song was loud and upbeat so I couldn't hear people asking for their checks.

The chorus was something like: "Masochists and sadists unite one and all, bondage is the rage, come on let's have a ball." Don't ask me why I was compelled at seventeen to write an S & M anthem. When I say it was upbeat, understand you still couldn't sing or dance to it . . . but I guess you could stand up and look like you were having some kind of seizure to it.

Hey, you gotta start somewhere. That was my first official stand-up gig, but my first paying gig was through a friend of mine, Alan Baral, who gave me $50 to perform at his school, Beaver College. Oh, how I wish I had gone there. It had been an all-girls school originally—you can't make this stuff up—and then it became coed, which is how Alan got me booked in their college lounge to perform some of the songs and comedy bits I did. I was supposed to do an hour but only had about eighteen minutes of material at that point: a couple comedy songs, originals and parodies—the highest form of comedy music behind lip-synching.

There was no light in the cafeteria lounge so I brought my own floodlight bulbs on a metal strip, which I pointed up at myself from the floor. It was lit like a horror film and played like one as well. Only someone coming up and throwing a bucket of blood on me would have given me a better closing. In 2001, Beaver College changed its name to Arcadia University. I believe I had everything to do with that.

So that was the beginning of it all, the illustrious start to my life on the comedy stage. And for the next ten years or so, from the age of seventeen to about twenty-seven, I tried to make a career out of it.

In that time I watched some of my peers become big successes and others fall by the wayside. Always a nice expression: *fell by the wayside.* In some cases, people fell off because they didn't have what it took, but often they were doing many of the right things but events beyond their control just hit them out of nowhere, like lightning hitting a tree in a thunderstorm. Or lightning hitting *you* in a thunderstorm.

Growing up in Norfolk I had a friend named B. J. Leiderman who was hit by lightning when he was eight years old. He survived. I actually just spoke to him for the first time in forty-four years. I wanted to confirm I had the facts right. As I said earlier, everybody should write a book—it's great, you get to talk to people you knew when you were eight.

I knew B. J. from riding the bus together to Hebrew school since we were five. And we weren't even Jewish, we just wanted to meet young Jewish girls. Our bus driver was Mr. Wilson, and when I was bad he would pinch my butt as hard as he could so I would stop misbehaving and sit down. I realize now that was child abuse. But he's long gone and so are the bruises. And between us, I don't have much of an ass at all, so if he tried that now, he'd be grabbing ass bone.

And even if I did have any meat on my ass today that he was able to grab ahold of right here and now, Mr. Wilson is sadly dead, so he would have to be a zombie to grab my ass, and that just wouldn't happen, because I would get away from him before he could get near my ass, 'cause—and I know it's not popular-culture speak—but I fucking hate zombies. I used to love the band the Zombies, my fave song of theirs being "Time of the Season." When I hear it, it takes me back to my Bar Mitzvah days.

For those of you who don't know what a Bar Mitzvah is, it's when a boy with a young girl's voice becomes a man. Then there's a *Bra* Mitzvah, which is when a thirteen-year-old girl becomes endowed with breasts ahead of her friends. And that is indeed a mitzvah (good deed). To have curves ahead of the curve.

As you may be able to tell, I did not have sex until I was seventeen. I was a troubled, lonely teen. Up until about the age of nine, I still had my mojo. But after that, it was all downhill for a long, long time. Nine was the perfect age for me. I was pseudo-popular, being a mixture of funny and obnoxious, and didn't yet have the complication of fluids coming out of me that I had almost no control over. All this leads to how comedy was my salvation.

At seventeen, the first joke I ever actually wrote was one that sums up the comedy I still find funny today, dark absurdist humor. I was a huge Monty Python fan, so the joke was basically something I'd gotten from just ingesting everything they did. I was an awkward seventeen-year-old when I wrote this down, onto actual lined paper, and it became one of the staples of my first five minutes as a starting comedian.

The joke goes: "I have the brain of a German shepherd and the body of a sixteen-year-old boy . . . and they're both in the trunk of my car and I want you to see them."

No reason to analyze it, it was what it was. If you had read that in the newspaper, that a sixteen-year-old boy and a German shepherd were in the trunk of my car, and me being barely older than sixteen myself . . . well, that would make me a suspect. Not good for my reputation. But in the context of stand-up it made people laugh. (Today, it would be no more than a tweet that some people would go "eww" over and others would type back "What?" to.)

Upon further watching and reading comedy years later I discovered that the joke was, for all intents and purposes, derived from a Groucho Marx line: "I've got the brain of a four-year-old. I'll bet he was glad to be rid of it." It wasn't intentional by any means and I didn't even comprehend the joke until years later, but it was a start.

By freshman and sophomore year in college, I would take the train from Philly to New York and sign up on the twelve-hour wait lists to go on at the famed Improv and Catch a Rising Star clubs. That train ride built character. I was the kid with a dream—and a really shitty guitar. Not quite a regular-sized guitar, not quite a ukulele, kind of a Shetland guitar. Being such a freakish instrument, maybe it made my music seem larger in scope than it was. Right, no, it did not.

The next few years I spent in college at Temple University. I worked in the deli to buy film stock, got myself a supportive girlfriend, and did sketch comedy at the neighboring University of Pennsylvania with my comedy partner, Sam Domsky, who is now a great dentist. Actually, I don't know if he's a great dentist. I know he's a funny dentist. Nitrous oxide story to come. Not involving Sam. Good dentists know good lawyers.

So to put it in a nutshell, which is what I call my sac, things started to take off toward the end of my college years—I was doing stand-up in Philly and getting onstage a lot at a club called Starz, owned by Stephen Starr (who is now one of the premiere restaurateurs of both Philly and New York). Stephen is really the first person of note that thought I was funny and gave me my start. You can blame him.

Most significantly at that time, I made a documentary about my nephew called *Through Adam's Eyes* which went on to win the Student Academy Award in 1978. The Student Academy Award is exactly the same as the Academy Award except the Oscar has acne.

The film was about my nephew Adam, who underwent reconstructive face surgery. He didn't need the operation. I made him get it because I wanted to make a film about it and win the Student Academy Award. That's what a selfish narcissist prick I was at twenty-one. No, of course that's not what happened.

My nephew Adam had a genetic birth defect and they rebuilt his face by taking ribs out of his chest and using them to construct new cheekbones. Adam was seven when the film was made and he narrated it. It's really his film, embodied by his charm and intelligence and how he dealt with his young life's challenging circumstances. Adam and his perspective is the reason the film got some notice.

I traveled back to L.A. to accept the award, and while I was in town I went on at the Comedy Store, where owner Mitzi Shore said I could be a regular if I wanted to be one. I was very excited. I was already planning to go to USC grad film school, but I decided instead to drop out and focus on stand-up. Mitzi's offer was generous: I could work for free, and I didn't even have to sleep with her. She was like an aunt to me. An aunt I didn't have to sleep with.

I did what you do to work at being a stand-up—getting any stage time I could and playing nonpaying gigs in L.A. while also getting sets at the Improv, thanks to Budd Friedman, to hone my skills and build my reputation—and then began my journey to start working on the road.

I had a strong closer with my Shetland guitar. My big finish for several years was playing George Harrison's "While My Guitar Gently Weeps" while turning a valve on a shampoo bottle filled with water, hidden behind the pegs, electric-taped to a garden hose with holes cut throughout its length.

As I sang the most civilian version of the epic song imaginable, water poured through the holes in the garden hose and my pants ended up drenched at the end. I would look at the audience, pants soaking wet, and say to a guy in the front, "My pants are wet, and it's your fault." That's right, a musical prop bit ending with wetting *someone else*'s pants—I'd sunk as low as a kid with a dream could sink. Of course it was a real audience pleaser.

Except in giant venues. I got a few bigger gigs, like in Tahoe at Harrah's opening for the great Kenny Loggins, and the audience could barely see the water cascading from my guitar. Even with backlighting, it wasn't very visible. The other dilemma was the floor was soaked, and one time in true newbie fashion, I grabbed the mic stand after the song to say goodnight and got an electric shock because I was standing in the puddle I'd created. I retired that closing bit a couple years later after playing some smaller clubs with carpeted stages.

To give you an idea of how crappy a road gig can be when you're just starting out, here's a sordid tale of one of my first. It was a club in Anchorage, Alaska, that was actually a strip club, but comics got to go on in between the strippers. I went there, at the suggestion of Jay Leno, with Kevin Nealon and another comedian who I know would like to remain nameless. Kevin and I visited all the tourist sites of Alaska—we were like two men on a honeymoon—while the other comic stayed in the trailer with the strippers. He may have made the right decision.

Apparently, it was not a criminal offense to possess pot and guns at that time in Alaska, so the audiences were two things a lot of Americans to this day enjoy being: stoned and armed. There was a stripper with pie pans on her breasts and one over her groinal area. She danced around, lit matches taped to her pie pans, blew them all out, then announced, "And now, please welcome the comedy of Bob Saget!" I came onstage to the smells of sulfur and stripper sweat, and proceeded to talk to the audience about my relationship with my girlfriend. I thought I heard a gun being cocked, but in retrospect it may have just been the sound of my shitting myself.

Things didn't get much easier as I tried to move forward in the comedy world. I toured with the Comedy Store College Tour, which meant I played a lot of lunch cafeterias with two other comedians, Jeff DeHart and Fred Raker. I was also fortunate to become the audience warm-up comedian for the sitcom *Bosom Buddies*, as I'd become friends with the producer and writer, Chris Thompson. Even got to appear on the show once as "Bob the Comic," as I was dubbed by Tom Hanks, since the writers had made me the generic young comic with no name.

By this point it was the early eighties and I lived in a single apartment in Palms. That is, until that fateful day when a shotgun was found in the pool. I decided to move out—just didn't feel like a safe place to live anymore. Made that decision without the help of counsel. I was in my early twenties, young and lost. Those two things often go together.

I'd met my future managers in Buffalo while on the college tour and decided to sign with them—they liked me. They thought I was funny. And yet I still trusted them. They were successful in the live music business, so it made sense to me. I was twenty-one, living in L.A., and they were in Buffalo, New York—Brad Grey and Harvey Weinstein. Back then, they were not very well-known. Today, they are very well-known.

Even though the early eighties and the comedy scene were sometimes a blur of drugs and booze, I remember everything and everyone from those early struggling comic days. But one person who stands out most is Rodney Dangerfield. I met him in

1980 when I was in La Jolla for the weekend doing stand-up at the Comedy Store. I'd just gotten offstage and Rodney walked in with two women on his arms. He came up to me and said, "You're funny, man. I saw you on *Merv Griffin*." I was pretty excited and my ego was starting to engorge, when he proceeded to sum me up in a couple sentences: "You got a funny Jew head, man—you're fucked—your mind is always going. Better to be born rich, dumb, and Catholic." (Or words to that effect.)

Then he went on to tell me he'd tried to go to La Costa, a health spa resort near San Diego, to clean out. He'd only lasted there for one day. "I can't do it, man," he said. "No booze, no coke, no pot, no pills." He kept repeating that as a mantra of sorts. Funny as hell.

I was excited to meet this man who'd made me laugh for years, an icon, and one whose whole image and attitude was that of an outcast. I think that's why I and so many other people could relate to Rodney and his true feeling of a lack of "respect." He was always encouraging to me. He was encouraging to a lot of other young comics as well. And he never touched me.

It was that year, 1980, that Rodney exploded into the comedy film world with *Caddyshack*. He was fifty-nine when the movie came out. Fifty-nine. I'll say that once more with feeling. Fifty-nine. That's how long he did stand-up and struggled to get his name known, before his first successful movie.

I am majorly inspired by Rodney's timeline. From being born Jacob Cohen in 1921 to getting "no respect" his whole life, and then rising to worldwide recognition just before he turned sixty . . . no wonder he felt tortured. I got to know him well. Perhaps too well. He was a complex man, but an incredibly funny man, and he loved young comedians more than almost anyone. He identified with their struggle.

In 1980, when I first met him at the club, I ended up hanging out that whole weekend with him. I remember he wore linen pants and a shirt held together by only two buttons. That was his outfit, and he wore that as much as he wore his work uniform: the signature black suit, white shirt, and red tie.

I stayed friends with him for many years, until the end of his life. Officiated his funeral. A funeral where the pallbearers were me, Rodney's son Brian, his son-in-law David, producer David Permut, comedian Harry Basil, Jim Carrey, Michael Bolton, Rob Schneider, and Adam Sandler. I was honored to officiate. It's something I was unfortunately experienced at handling. I had been asked to officiate by his wife, Joan, and I wanted to be there for his children, Melanie and Brian.

After all the stuff my family had been through, a lot of my friends over the years knew I was pretty good at dealing with death, that I could make people laugh even at the most difficult times. Not necessarily something I'd want to boast about: "Man, my grandmother's funeral was hilarious! And the deli was delicious!" But as Rodney always said, "It is what it is." If I can help others laugh and ease their pain at a traumatic time in their lives, it is an honor.

By the way, what is it with Jewish people—of which I am one—and deli food at the most emotional moments? Deli at a funeral, deli at a circumcision . . . I still can't get over the image of my cousin's baby having his penis clipped in front of a hundred people, and then someone coming in with a deli plate with pounds of tongue majorly featured. On the very same spot: penis and tongue. Go together like hand and glove. If the glove had one finger.

But let me get back to Rodney for a moment. It's not fair for me to just open with "This is how I met him" and then "He was buried." He had a style all his own. He was competitive: he wanted to have the funniest jokes that ever existed and lay them out in a way that sideswiped you because they were so hilarious and delivered in such a rapid-fire style that you were almost body-punched into laughing.

His style was also to make fun of himself. He would say things like, "I got no opening, I got no close, and I'm weak in the middle." Not all comedians are meant to take this self-deprecating approach. But his philosophy was that you had to take shots at yourself before taking shots at anyone else. I could relate. I definitely had a bit of Rodney in me—again, not literally.

But he gave me a lot of advice. One of the most valuable things he ever said to me was: "Just go like a tank. Just go straight ahead and keep goin'. They wanna stop you. Nobody wants to help you. Just go forward . . . like a tank." I say that same metaphor to younger comedians today when they ask me for advice.

Rodney was very helpful to young comedians, and it was largely because he'd gone through so many hard times himself. As I mentioned before, he hosted *The Ninth Annual Young Comedians Special,* where I appeared with many "beginning" comedians, including Sam Kinison, whom I'd met in Houston while doing stand-up. That was just after the time Sam had chained himself to a telephone pole in front of a comedy club and appeared in the *Houston Chronicle* wearing a crown of thorns and a diaper, saying the club had persecuted him like Jesus.

A few years later, Sam and I would occasionally hang out late into the night at the Comedy Store in L.A. I remember once the two of us were sitting at a table on Sunset Boulevard, Sam with a bottle of Jack, and he looked up at me and said, "Bob, do you ever get depressed?" I said, "Yeah, Sam." He asked, "Do you drink when you're depressed?" I said, "Yeah, sometimes." He told me, "Next time you get depressed, you come see me." I loved his comedy mind, but let's just say he wouldn't have been the first person I'd have gone to when I got depressed. And I got depressed a lot.

Drowning my sorrows in booze wasn't my style. And I want to go on record that I'm anti-drugs, except the ones I take for cholesterol, anxiety, a sleep disorder, and tranquilizing animals.

I don't smoke pot anymore. Used to in my early twenties. Hard to avoid it if you're around comedians and musicians. And restaurant employees. And heart surgeons. I'm not much into it anymore, but I do think pot is overly criticized. Especially bad pot. The smell of bad pot is necessary. It helps you appreciate the smell of good pot.

Once when I was back in Philadelphia visiting my parents, I tried to get my dad to sneak away from my mom and smoke with me. Told him it would open up his mind. He didn't do it. Mainly because he was afraid of the smoke that would go into his lungs. Since his heart attacks, he'd stopped smoking permanently many years earlier. Also he regarded marijuana as a drug that made you lose control of your mind. And he didn't need that. His mind was already controlled. By my mother.

I didn't even start smoking until I moved to Los Angeles in my twenties. Thinking about it now, it served its purpose for me. Especially while I was on the road and getting through the struggle that comes with what Lenny Bruce called "having twenty-three hours to kill" after that one hour onstage at night. Not the healthiest lifestyle choice.

Nor was cocaine, which I also tried in the early eighties but learned pretty quickly that it destroys all passages, whether they be nasal, heart, or life. And the real problem for a comedian on cocaine at two A.M., besides the triple-time heartbeats, is the loss of appetite.

Throughout the constant struggle and rejection I must say that fun times were had during those years—hanging out with comedians at every deli in L.A. or New York at two A.M., eating hot pastrami sandwiches. Some of those comedians, amazingly, are still alive. By morning, pink pastrami juice was sweating out of our pores. That shit can kill you. You know the old joke "How do you get to Carnegie Hall?" "Practice"? For some comedians the goal was just getting to Carnegie Deli.

It's funny the things I end up remembering most about those years. I guess defining moments for a struggling young comedian come in many forms. For some the motivation is just to get laid. That wasn't really my motivation for most of my up-and-not-coming years because I had a girlfriend, whom I ended up getting married to. But for others, it was everything.

Getting laid and doing stand-up are inextricably linked. Even just the sight of a man or woman alone onstage can have a sexual element to it. There's no way the audience can look at this one person up there for an hour or more and not end up checking them out. Even if the response is nausea. Some comedians today go way past being monologists by wearing the tightest jeans they can and gyrating like a Cirque du Soleil performer. You use whatever works for you.

There's a school of newish (not usually Jewish) comedians today who are very physical. It's almost like you're watching them do martial arts while they're telling jokes. It works for me if the story they're telling is *about* martial arts, but otherwise, I am drawn toward comedians with more humanlike behavior. Anything that steals focus from the artist that's not organic to what they're saying makes it harder for me to connect.

Sam Kinison had a funny physical bit about having sex with his wife—about how she would buzzkill him while he was trying to have sex with her by bringing up errands and daily chores he had to do for her. He would disconnect the mic as though it was his dick and mime being behind his wife. He'd thrust himself toward the audience, miming as if she was in front of him, and yell at the back of her head, "Come on, let's do this . . . ah, that's good, baby." And then she'd kill his buzz: "We've gotta fix the fence. It needs another coat of paint." Then he'd go off: "Can we talk about this later?! I'M TRYING TO FUCK YOU . . ." And then he'd scream: "AHHHHHHHHHHGGGHHHH!!!!!"

I never made a decision to be a dirty-bastard comedian. I just did then—and do now—what I find funny. I like entertaining families too. Man, does that read oddly. Over the years my sick litany of humor may be blue at times, but predominantly, it's just silly. There's a time and place for cursing. And I never wanted to do it just arbitrarily for shock value. Fuck.

Sam was just one of the many interesting people I had the fortune of knowing in those years. It's amazing how many of us came up through that circuit, doing spots at the Comedy Store and the Improv, and the other clubs in L.A. that started lots of us as well, the Comedy and Magic Club and the Ice House. And later, the Laugh Factory. Always memorable names. They were more than just nightclubs, they were stores that were open for business based on the premise that you would pay some money to the owner and you would be compensated with laughter. That's not a bad trade. Just entertainment. Simple in theory, but complicated when a lot of people who'd perform in New York and L.A. wanted a career break so they'd never have to work in those places again.

There came a time when all my peers seemed to be "graduating," getting their own television shows and movies, while I was stuck doing the same thing, hosting the Comedy Store, doing spots at the Improv, getting occasional gigs on the road.

This was during the big comedy boom when Robin Williams was about to do *Laugh-In 2* and Michael Keaton was cast with Jim Belushi in a CBS show, *Working Stiffs*. For a period, it felt like I was never going to get "out of the clubs." Every couple months another one of my comedy friends was becoming a breakout star . . . Arsenio Hall, Howie Mandel, Garry Shandling. Not to mention the earlier comedians I'd only just met in the clubs who were already popping off to the next stage of their careers: Robin, Keaton, Billy Crystal, David Letterman.

David was always kind to me. I even offered him the option of sleeping with my cousin Joyce, because I'd heard they'd gone out once. He seemed to like earnest younger comedians who worked hard and had an original voice and dignity. And I could never have displayed more dignity than I did when I offered him my cousin to sleep with.

As smarmy as the atmosphere often was, I somehow knew I was in the right place to learn from all these funny people, but I always felt ten years behind schedule. And that kind of thinking can keep you there. You gotta do what Rodney said, "Just go like a tank." You can't care about someone else's career path. If anything, I was at my best during those struggling years when I was sincerely happy for my peers' successes, not walking around like a loser late at night, being fed by the negative patter of comedians out of work: "How'd he get that?" "Why wasn't I submitted for that?" "They wanted him over me?" "I hate my agent." "You're lucky you have one." All negative commentary, all said to this day standing outside of comedy clubs around the world. And none of it moves anyone forward.

It's all about timing. I may have been remotely likable, but I didn't have the high-energy performance combined with the kind of material that I knew could've set me apart. It's almost like I chose to make the life of a stand-up and the many thousands of sets onstage—just the whole thing itself—the best takeaway from all those years.

I don't regret it. I learned something very simple and significant in those years: I loved doing comedy. I loved watching things I'd introduce one night turn into something much funnier a few days later. A craft it is. Just like acting, writing, and slicing deli. Slicing deli is actually regarded as a trade, but I will always look at it as a craft.

There are many exciting art forms enveloped by show business. I love many of them as much as I do stand-up. But stand-up comedy does something unique. It allows an artist to go onstage alone; weave together all their writings, thoughts, feelings, and emotions;

and then share them live, directly with an audience. There is nothing like a stand-up audience. Because there is nothing like a stand-up.

This feels frighteningly like I am about to spontaneously burst into a comedian's sound-alike anthem version of "God Bless the USA." So in that vein, I'd like to dedicate this chapter to all our young women and men around this entire planet, out there every day, risking their lives and presence of mind, selflessly bringing laughs into the hearts of millions of human beings who need to laugh so badly.

Bill Cosby said it pretty eloquently: "Through humor, you can soften some of the worst blows that life delivers. And once you find laughter, no matter how painful your situation might be, you can survive it."

And once you have survived the difficult times in your life, if you choose to, and have that gift, you can channel them through stand-up. And then you can proudly, and with no shame at all, tell your audience things like: My newest Grammy-nominated stand-up comedy special, *That's What I'm Talkin' About*, is available now on iTunes, Amazon, and Netflix. God Bless America.

Chapter 5

AS ONE DOOR OPENS

I will never forget my first time on *The Tonight Show Starring Johnny Carson*. In all my appearances with the TV legend, I never did straight stand-up, just paneled with him and tried to weave in my comedy as stories in the conversation, which he was a master of. So on my first appearance on *The Tonight Show*—well, first appearance with Johnny (I had appeared once previously with guest host Garry Shandling)—I talked about this real dream I'd had with Johnny in it, a dream about us in a limo together.

He found the story compelling, apparently, and had me back numerous times, always treating me with great respect. At the time, with more than I imagined I deserved. I couldn't believe I was actually on Johnny's show. I'd watched him my whole life, just loving his humor, his style, and the comedians he enjoyed having on, never even considering the possibility I'd be a stand-up one day.

I find it fascinating that I just wrote the words *I'd watched him my whole life*. People come up to me and say "I've watched you my whole life" and they are sixteen. That is their whole life. Then I shake their hand and feel my elbow crack and think to myself, Holy shit, Bob, you are really not sixteen anymore.

I remember when I was only eleven and had a poignant moment, as a viewer, watching Johnny on New Year's Eve. I was staying in Washington, DC, visiting my cousin Tootsie—that's right—and her husband, Jules. They had a dinner party to go to so I stayed home in their beautiful apartment near the Capitol with my aunt Becky. She was actually my dad's first cousin but was so old I called her "aunt" out of respect.

I knew it was going to be a rough evening because I was going to have to sleep in Aunt Becky's room, and she was a giant snorer. So I stayed as long as possible in the den watching the entire *Tonight Show*. It was ninety minutes long then. Johnny made my night. He brought in the New Year for me. I'm not sure I recall correctly, but I believe he lit a sparkler and then made fun of it, saying that was all the show had in the budget for fireworks.

When I finally went into Aunt Becky's room, she was asleep and I arrived to a chamber of THX sounds the scope of a George Lucas film. She was in one single bed and I was in another—I crawled into my bed but couldn't sleep; the snoring was insane. So I used my resources, grabbed a couple tissues, balled them up in my ears, and to secure them, put a ski mask over my head. All was good. I laid my head down to sleep but suddenly had to sneeze . . .

The volume of my eruption woke Aunt Becky out of her Snuffleupagus coma, and when her head sprang up at exactly the same time my head came up, she screamed at the sight of this person next to her in a ski mask. I started to yell, *"No, Aunt Becky, it's me!"* and grabbed the ski mask to pull it off, but that only made her scream more. It was quite a scene.

She didn't have a heart attack, though she may have soiled herself. Eventually things calmed down and we both went to bed. It was a memorable night, but what stuck with me above all else from that New Year's was having watched Johnny Carson. That's the thing about late-night TV like Johnny—as a viewer you feel an intimacy, like you have a personal relationship with him. Not creepy if you accept the whole host–audience broadcasting premise.

From then on I was a huge fan of Johnny Carson and by the time I was sixteen I was watching him every night—and his frequent guest, the beyond-hilarious Don Rickles. Of course, I never dreamed that I would be so fortunate as to have Don as a dear friend today, that this icon would be someone whom I now have dinner with and revere as I would my own father. With the exception that if I was at a dinner with my own father, I wouldn't be subject to Don's famous ridicule and told over and over again how little I mean to him.

All right, sorry, these damn tangents, back to the dream about Johnny Carson that I shared with him on the air . . .

So I'm on *The Tonight Show*, telling Johnny about my limo dream: I was in the passenger seat, Johnny was driving. He politely acted intrigued that I'd made him the driver. In the backseat were comedian Buddy Hackett, legendary drummer (and friend of Johnny's) Buddy Rich, and actor Buddy Ebsen (Jed Clampett, Barnaby Jones). Three Buddies. Only a comic can dream in alliteration. I turned to Johnny, telling him and the audience, "This is true . . ." I said that a lot. And Johnny responded the way he did with most stories I'd tell him by saying, "I don't care if it's true or not, just tell it already."

So as the dream goes, we drove into a ditch and water was

pouring in and close to covering our heads. We would've drowned, except I saved everyone, Johnny first. He said, "Uhh, thank you very much." And then, in order, I saved Buddy Hackett, Buddy Rich, and went back much later for Buddy Ebsen. I looked into the camera and said, "Sorry, Mr. Ebsen." Then I turned back to Johnny and said, "Then we all went back to your house and you gave us your robes, slippers, and pajamas to put on and we sat around and had milk and cookies."

Didn't take a therapist to figure out I wanted to be accepted into show business. Many years and appearances later, Johnny had me on, for the last time, just two weeks before he left the show entirely. On that night I'd given him an engraved watch, thanking him for his "thirty years of great service." He seemed visibly touched—until I whipped out another dozen watches and started handing them out to Ed McMahon, Doc Severinsen, the band, and later, Bill Cosby. Bill came out and said, "I want one of those watches," so I gave one to him, and he stood at the center of the stage and stomped on it with his foot.

All in all, I was on *The Tonight Show* with Johnny thirteen times. After one appearance, Johnny passed my mother and father backstage and politely listened to my mom say, "It's so nice to meet you. We think you've been doing a *very* good job." Thanks, Mom. Man had been the king of television for thirty years and Dolly Saget thought he was doing a *very* good job. But he was the king. And my mother was, and still is, Dolly Saget.

So for around a decade I was floating as a panel guest with thirteen appearances on Johnny, and roughly the same number with David Letterman, and also with Conan O'Brien. I count talk show appearances like Rain Main counts lines in the sidewalk. In my early twenties, some of the first television I ever did was *The Merv Griffin Show*. Thirteen times on that one. Ask any comedian when they're starting out how many times they've been on a talk show and they'll know the exact number. Merv was very kind to me. He never touched me either. I've been relatively unscathed. Merv was very good to comics, as was Johnny. I appeared once on *The Mike Douglas Show* from Philadelphia but only because I was an intern on the show during college.

Any time I reflect like this on showbiz things from the past I feel like I'm dating myself. Well, at this moment in the book writing process I *am* dating myself. I'm gonna get to second base tonight. Second base is still "copping a feel," right? I get to second base every time I say the Pledge of Allegiance. Or take a shower. Or massage my tits. Until they lactate. That's always an unexpected buzzkill.

What's third and fourth base now? Third used to be something involving fingers, and fourth was going all the way. I think fourth now is anal sex while both people are standing in front of a jet engine. That should be third base and then you could get your head blown off while you're getting your head blown off. Best way to go—ever. I'd be shocked if anyone doesn't flat-out agree with me on that one.

But back to *The Tonight Show*. Of course I didn't just *wind up* on Johnny Carson's show. There were a couple beats in between, during my early struggling comedian days. Stand-up is hard and success is elusive. But back in 1986, I had finally started to feel like the eight years of comedy on the road, and thousands of sets at the Comedy Store and the Improv, had begun to pay off. Especially when I got to work with Richard Pryor, in a Paramount movie called *Critical Condition*. He inspired me beyond words. Silly to type that, right? I mean, he was Richard Pryor.

But before I got to work with Richard on that film, I'd spent many weekends hosting at the Comedy Store seeing him perform and getting to know him a little. He was already a big star. I mean, again, he was Richard Pryor. One night my spot was bumped because Richard had decided to go on. To make me feel better, he asked me if I wanted to go outside and see his new Testarossa. I was dumb, didn't know it was the name of a car. Thought he was making a joke, like he was gonna show me his dick on Sunset Boulevard.

Many years later, when he started to succumb to multiple sclerosis, I visited him at his house, where I had the honor of getting to hang out with him a little. We spent the time watching his new wide-screen rear-projection TV together. It was hard to see one of my heroes in that state—such an amazing talent. I saw him a couple times after that, and the last time was not long before he died, at a shoot for a Showtime pilot that Eddie Griffin was portraying Richard in.

I went upstairs at the location to see him and gave him a hug. His MS had taken away most of his physical control, but he was still there. As I walked upstairs, I noticed Pat O'Brien was in the building and *Access Hollywood* was filming every moment surrounding Richard. I whispered something in Richard's ear so the cameras couldn't hear. A couple days later, when the program aired, they showed me whispering in close-up while synthesizer strings played in the background. The narration said ". . . and Bob Saget was one of the few people to make Richard laugh that day."

What I'd whispered in his ear was that my youngest daughter

couldn't sleep the night before, so she came into my room and lay in bed next to me. My issue was I'd been having diarrhea that night. So I described to Richard how I was afraid all night that I was going to shit the bed with her in it. He started to laugh, so I kept describing my paranoia of blasting my bowels all over the walls, like spin art. Explosive diarrhea, my A-game.

I wish I'd spent more time with him and been able to say I was an actual "friend" of Richard's. A lot of people who work with legends like Pryor tend to spew out what good "friends" they are with them. Richard Pryor was an icon to me. He was the King. A significant mentor also—especially after the three weeks I spent with him in High Point, North Carolina, shooting *Critical Condition*. He let me in to hang a little bit and know and learn from him. I know some of the people who were his true friends. And they were fortunate people. I was fortunate to just know the man and have the time I got to spend with him.

I had some very memorable conversations with Richard during my three weeks of shooting in High Point. We were hiding in a hospital alcove waiting to be cued. There was a bit of time to kill. One of those scrubbing pads was on a medical tray in the room with us. It had a soft side like one you clean pots with and on its other side, hard plastic bristles. Richard pointed at it and said, "You see this side," indicating the hard bristle side, "That's the side they took my skin off with after the fire." There was no laughing to be had, just a discussion about pain. And then we were needed in the scene, so the switch was flipped to go back to work. I was struck by what a hardcore and yet gentle man he was.

The scene we were about to do wasn't intended to have any laughs in it. Richard and I were *in places*, and there was this dead guy being wheeled by us on a gurney. My line as the young Dr. Joffe was something like "They found this guy washed up in the drink." I can't remember it, but it was about the bloated dead actor on the gurney. I had to deliver the line to Richard and every time I looked at the drenched guy on the gurney I laughed my ass off. I mean, he was a wet bloated dead guy on a gurney. I was in character for all the other scenes, but every time I looked at this dead guy and then up to Richard to deliver the line, I lost it. Then he lost it. I think it was like twenty takes. The director, Michael Apted, could not have been more patient.

One of the things I asked Richard, which I've asked a lot of comedians, is: "When did you know you were funny?" Richard said, "I was four." I related to that because that's when I knew it too. And yes, I am aware I was in the presence of Richard Pryor. I know I will never be that great a stand-up and would never presume that I am. He was a comedic genius. I realize it was like asking Albert Einstein "if he liked ice cream too." I was just excited that I shared that with him, that we both thought we were funny at four years old.

Flashing back, only one year after I did that movie with Richard, I was certain I would never work in show business again. I'd been back in Los Angeles from High Point, and at that time in my life, working in a Paramount film with Pryor was itself a *high point*. Had a few stand-up gigs, but the phone didn't ring much. Okay, it did, but it was my mother.

The stereotypical neurotic unhealthy show business cliché is that you work in something good and then assume, during the quiet times that follow, you will never work again. A bit extreme, but it can happen, and when it's years between significant gigs, it feels like forever. The key during those times is to just live your life, be a human first, and not let show business define you. It's also helpful during the droughts of nonwork to not get hit by a bus.

So during the six months that followed the release of the film, the movie hadn't yet led to bigger things like I had hoped. But on the brighter, human, more important, *life* side of a comedian/actor's fucked-up psyche, I had just gotten married to my high school girlfriend and we were going to have our first child.

I'd been told a new baby brings you luck and I still believe this to be true. Babies are so cute and positive. They are the human being we are meant to be before our environment corrupts and morphs us. Unless you're born a mean evil baby, which I've seen only a couple times. That's a drag. When you meet a *mean baby*, right? When you go over to the bassinet to look lovingly at the little bundle of joy and the kid gives you a glare that just says, "Fuck you." Now perhaps he just shit himself or hasn't been held in a while, but still . . . When you see a rotten negative little thing like that, it makes you believe in past lives, makes you think: What the hell happened to this mean little fucker at the end of his last incarnation? Mean little evil bastard baby. He'll be a wonderful agent one day.

While my wife was pregnant, my career started to gain steam. Again, not a life-affirming perspective, but many a comedian's mind-set before they've had therapy. Not only had I begun appearing every few months on *The Tonight Show* but I got a job on a CBS show called *The Morning Program* and moved to New York. I was hired as a kind of sidekick, appearing on the show every day from seven to nine A.M., same time as the *Today* show and *Good Morning America*. It was a huge break for me but I had a sense after four months that I might not last.

Part of this had to do with a very traumatic event that happened in my personal life. I debated whether or not to include it in the book, as it was truly one of the most nightmarish moments ever for me and my family. Especially for my ex-wife. Not to ruin the surprise for you, but I must tell you that it ended well. Very well. My ex-wife and I have been divorced since 1998. The good ending was having a healthy baby and her healthy mother.

Seriously, I wouldn't be telling this difficult story if I hadn't been given my ex-wife's and my oldest daughter's sanctions to do so. It seems like a lifetime ago. To be honest, until writing this book, I had not been able to fully give this incident thought or go to the place I was at when it all happened.

One of my revolving jokes that year was, "I married my girl-friend of seven years—that's her age." Well, it wasn't her age; she was my high school girlfriend. We got married in 1982 and in 1987 she was about to give birth to our first child. I took a leave of absence from *The Morning Program* as a paternity leave.

It all started with her having a difficult labor that wouldn't end. We went to the hospital as young excited parents, euphoric to have our first kid. We stayed up all night in a labor room and by the early morning she needed to have a C-section.

While they administered the epidural, they went into my wife's spinal column incorrectly with the needle and the meds went into her bloodstream. Please forgive my pedestrian medical translation here. From my best recollection, her heartbeat got very faint and slowed to the point where the anesthesiologist had to inject her with epinephrine (adrenaline). Her heart rate picked up—but it raced to a high of 180 and then suddenly flatlined. The hospital called a code blue and roughly thirty plainclothes doctors and nurses descended into the operating room. I was told to stand behind the green line on the floor.

The doctors pounded on her chest to bring her heartbeat back, and they succeeded. They stabilized her and put three different catheters into her heart, nose, and mouth to remove the fluids from the IV that had basically drowned her. At the same time, they operated and took my daughter safely out. I was only getting bits and pieces of information, as we do in these hospital crisis situations. One nurse told me my wife had no brain activity. At that moment I was standing alone in a hallway believing my wife was in a coma and that I might never see her or my new baby daughter.

I stood there in shock for a while until finally . . . I saw my daughter. They wheeled her out in a bassinet to take her to intensive care, as they do with traumatic births. She was also a bit jaundiced.

Though it was all happening as if in slow motion, I'll never forget the first moment I saw her. The nurse, who was wheeling her in a sealed incubator, was crying. She pulled it together and said to me as lucidly as she could, "This is your daughter." I remember looking at my baby and wanting to hold her—even though she was in the incubator—but also feeling like this was all a dream, like it was happening to someone else and I was just looking in.

My heart goes out to anyone who has gone through this. Or worse. I must share that this whole incident reinstilled in me a love for and faith in medical people—how they do their best and how even the most seemingly unsympathetic doctors and nurses are there for you emotionally when these horrific moments happen to people.

It felt like hours went by. They continued to stabilize my wife while I ran downstairs to the lobby to tell both sets of our parents what had happened. They hadn't let my new daughter's grand-parents come upstairs, so they were all four trapped in the lobby, panicked beyond belief. I remember their faces as I told them everything, their looks of horror—but also strength. I was the messenger.

My father's eyes welled up; he didn't say a word, but he looked at me with love and courage. It was the look I'd seen in his eyes too many times before throughout our lives. The look that said, "We will get through this." I'll remember for the rest of my life that look my father gave me. He gave it to me a lot. That's how you define what a great father is. That look.

I went back upstairs and spent another hour waiting. I was in the labor room where we had waited in presurgery during her labor, and I remember sitting there silently just praying. I was raised Jewish, but at that moment, I prayed to every deity that mankind has conjured. I prayed to God, Jesus, Buddha, Muham-mad, the Universe, Nothing, and I think I even mentioned Yoda. I prayed for my wife's life and for my daughter's life.

After what seemed like an eternity, I was standing outside the operating room as they finally wheeled out my wife, unconscious and wired up with the heart, throat, and nose catheters. Even though she was unconscious, I started talking to her, telling her everything I wanted to say: "You can't die . . . We just had a new baby and she's healthy . . ."

Nurses were standing around crying, I was crying, everyone was crying. Then, suddenly, in an instant, her eyes opened. She became fully conscious and agitated. The nurses called doctors over and everyone calmed her down, as of course, she was in shock. After a nightmare of harrowing proportions, a miracle had occurred.

I was able to see my daughter right away and give her Similac since her mom was in intensive care for several days recovering. I held the bottle at my chest as if I was really breast-feeding her, maybe thinking I could fake her out. I don't know why I did that. Traumatic situations sometimes call for odd behavior. I used to have a joke to that effect: "Men can breast-feed. I read that. Okay, I wrote it down and then I read it."

After six long difficult days at the hospital, my baby and her reincarnated mother were finally able to come home to our apartment. The trauma was over. What was left was healing and recovery. We had a live-in nurse for the next couple weeks and I was about to go back to work at the CBS show. We had been through hell and back. My wife and I would never be the same. But even in the darkest moments, humor always emerged. And as things started to get back to normal, the gallows-humor devils inside me were creeping back into my recovering psyche. Never appropriate, never printable, but always there. It's a twisted comic gene that's inbred in me, for better or for worse. And it didn't take long, post-trauma, for it to come out.

An old comic friend, whom I knew from my college days, when I did comedy at the University of Pennsylvania, Paul Provenza, and another friend, publicist Jackie Green, stopped by our apartment on the Upper West Side to say hi and see my new kid. They were the first visitors we'd had since both sets of grandparents had returned to Philly.

Paul and Jackie were only coming over for a moment. It was a very emotional, intimate moment; they had tears in their eyes as I came to the door holding my baby. Her mom was recovering, napping down the hall. Paul and Jackie walked into the entryway, their eyes filled with tears as they saw my new baby in my arms. Paul said, "She's very beautiful."

[FREEZE FRAME]

Now, this is hard to explain, but here's what followed. Please understand it came in the aftermath of a hugely traumatic event—and I am by nature a comedian who, as a defense against his own unbearable pain, goes straight to the most tasteless joke that can be conjured. I decide to share it here, as it's already been put into the ether. It was called out in print by a smart, stealthy writer, George Gurley, who did a story on me in the *New York Observer*, and as if that's not enough, it is featured inside the extras on the *Aristocrats* DVD.

Years later, I told my daughter the story before she had to read or hear about it. So by the time *The Aristocrats* came out, there was nothing she didn't know. I have three daughters—and they occasionally have the same sense of humor as me, but not in this case. What can I say. It's the sense of humor my father had handed down to me. It was an auto-response in the moment. Keep in mind that what I said to Paul Provenza that day—in response to his kind comment while I was holding my first child—came out because I was emotionally drained and had no filters at that instant. No filters at all. Okay, those are all the disclaimers I can think of.

[UN-FREEZE-FRAME]

So I'm holding my baby, we all have tears in our eyes, my wife is sleeping just down the hall, and we're back with Paul and Jackie where we left off. Paul looks at my baby in my arms and says, "She's very beautiful." And I (allegedly) auto-respond back . . .

"You can finger her for a dollar."

Time stopped. It was one of those gallows jokes that just spewed out. Apologies to the Universe. My poor-taste comedic response poked its irreverent head out of a sea of overwhelming relief warped through tears. The comment halted all three of us for a moment or two and then we broke out in laughter.

Paul Provenza, my houseguest that day, would eventually get older and become, decades later, the director of *The Aristocrats*. During those years, I often denied ever uttering that disgusting and unthinkable comment with the retort "I could never have said that. That's my daughter we are talking about here. It would've been at least for five dollars."

Anyway, this story traveled for years—not of my doing—among a sick group of comedy misanthropes. This is my breed's kind of jokey gossip. It's the humor of these dirty roasts some comedians do, where ethical people say the most reprehensible thing possible to make a point of how unthinkable and evil the actions described really are. It's an "honor among thieves" type of credo. And this kind of sick humor, comedy based on the worst circumstances in life a human being can go through, was the whole foundation of the movie *The Aristocrats*. But more on that later.

When I'm in certain comedy circles, my oldest daughter, who is now a brilliant twenty-seven-year-old artist, will be asked by other comedians, "Is that true?" And she smiles and nods her head affirmatively. She and her mother know me. And they know it's the farthest thing from reality. That's why they and other people close to me find the uncomfortable humor in it. They don't output that kind of humor, but they understand it.

So, I wasn't going to include that tale in this book, but my ex-wife said to me, "You *have* to. It's who you are. It's what the book is about. It's about how you and our family dealt with the unthinkable things that have happened."

I thank her for her encouragement and support in letting this one be told. To be clear and out of respect for her, understandably so, she did *not* sanction, at the time, my delivery of that particular punch line to Paul and Jackie. But she supported my telling the whole story now because it's representative of what this book is about.

Now, I would like to ask all of you reading this to please keep this story confidential and not share it with others. Let it be just between us. In confidence. Oh wait, this is in a book. Shit.

I have many friends in comedy who have told me, "You *have* to include that story in your book." Okay, I have. It's on all your heads now. My main concern was to tell it in a way that my daughter and her mother found palatable. It was a joke. And again, it couldn't be farther from who I am as a loving father. That is why it was found to be funny by some.

And like *The Aristocrats*, it is not for everyone. If I have offended anyone in the telling of this story, I apologize. I put it in here with as much context as I could. My heart goes out to anyone on this earth whom this is *not* an "in poor taste" joke to. Again, as my friend Rodney Dangerfield said, "It is what it is." And it was what it was.

So things got back to normal, life went on. Everyone was healthy. I went back to work at CBS. But I think I knew my days there were numbered when they offered to pick me up in a town car every morning at four fifteen A.M. to get *to* the show, but I'd have to find my own way back to my apartment *after* the show. One-way wannabe stardom at its best. I started to act out on the air. Not very professional but I was a kid, right?

One morning, the host of the show, Mariette Hartley, asked me, "Bob, are you a type-A personality?" My retort was, "Yes, but I'm trying to work on my A-ness." She told me, on the air, "Go to your room, Bob." My *room* was a fictional one we'd joke about on the show that was part of the set behind us. I walked upstage and up a set of stairs that led to nowhere. I stood there for maybe ten minutes, until the commercial break. The fuse had been lit. In showbiz they call that a "mutual parting of ways." I called it "two staircases that led to nowhere."

I remember my then-manager and still dearest friend, Brad Grey, sitting with me in executive producer Bob Shanks's office when Shanks—the man who had discovered me in the first place to give me this big shot on morning TV—had to break the news to me: The higher-ups at CBS wanted me out. What I didn't know until a couple weeks after the firing was that Brad had already been working to help me screen-test for a pilot for a network family sitcom on ABC called *Full House*.

I wasn't the first choice for the role of Danny Tanner. Betty White was. Not true, but there was another actor whom they had shot the pilot with. And upon seeing the pilot I thought he had done a really good job in it. I actually didn't understand why they wanted to replace him. The executive producer, Jeff Franklin, said it was because he'd always wanted me for the part but I wasn't available, since I was in New York doing *The Morning Program*.

Jeff Franklin and executive producers Tom Miller and Bob Boyett were about to change my life again. I will always be grateful for that monumental change.

I still have some guilt attached to the whole thing regarding the actor let go, though it was none of my doing. That's the unhealthy Jewish guilt that can haunt a person for no reason. Even if they're not Jewish. Even Catholic guilt can be blamed on Jewish guilt. I feel bad about that.

A great actor friend of mine, Joe Mantegna, whom I'd been lucky enough to also work with in *Critical Condition,* gave me some advice: "The minute you get fired from a job in New York, and they aren't paying you anymore . . . move." He was right. The cost of living there was high. I calculated it out—it equaled throwing a dollar bill into a bucket every fifteen minutes. Doesn't sound like much today. But it was for me back then. I'd just been fired from my first job in television.

I adore New York, and I'd love to live there again in my life, but it was time to leave. With a now-living wife and a healthy happy baby under my arm, who'd finally stopped crying, we packed up and moved back to Los Angeles.

Chapter 6

PARENTING MY OWN AND OTHER PEOPLE'S KIDS

So far in my life, I have three daughters—that I know of. I love them all equally and immensely. Okay, one of them is my favorite, but I cannot reveal which one until this book is in its incredibly large second printing. Actually, as most people who have more than one kid will tell you, there usually isn't a favorite. Your favorite is the one you're with that moment. I am beyond lucky in being able to play such a significant part in raising these three great young women. My daughters are really savvy and smart. They rarely curse, and they're not dirty ignorant people. They are dignified. How did they spring off from me, you may ask?

They actually reinforce my self-respect. They never judge me for anything I say onstage or in my work, even when it could embarrass them. I'm the only hypocrite in the family. I really want to be a good parent but I know it's a double-edged sword. How can I tell them to watch their language one minute, and the next minute I'm onstage talking about diarrhea and prison sex? Simultaneously.

Hey, shit happens. Especially in prison. When you're being triple-teamed like a pot of fondue boiling over on the stove. I pray this passage doesn't come before the grand jury of transitions . . . so, back to my daughters . . .

One of my daughters believes I'm like Benjamin Button, so by the time I'm ninety-five, I will be one year old. I'll need to be wiped again when I'm an old man, just like when I was a kid. Like in one of my friend Dana Carvey's best bits, where he portrays an angry old man yelling, "Wipe me! Wipe me!" as though he is once again pre-toilet-trained.

Truthfully, I'd never want that job to have to be done by anyone. Especially by offspring. I like the roles the way they are: "I'm the dad, and you're supposed to grow up and come to me for stuff when you need me." I like that kind of setup. And yet, with old age comes a return to innocence, which also leads to incontinence. And that's if you're lucky to live a long time. My dream is to live a really long time, just long enough to start pooping my pants and then get taken out before the shit really hits the proverbial fan.

When I was cast as a father on *Full House*—as a conservative, neurotic widowed father of three girls living in San Francisco—I admit I was surprised to land the role. Given my stand-up at the time, which to put it mildly always had a quirkiness to it, you'd think I'd have been cast as a guy who appears to be normal but then goes off the deep end and winds up cooking and eating people.

In today's television climate, that's certainly where we seem to be headed. Or be-headed. Must. Get. Viewers. "Tomorrow, on NBC—*Cannibal Father:* He loves his family so much, he cuts them up and *eats* them." The theme song could go: "Everywhere you look, there's a hand to hack on to . . ."

As I've been writing, lots of people have asked me, "What's your book gonna be about?" My go-to answer's been: "My book's about death, comedy, my testicles, and how they all intersect." The blank stares have been deafening. Then a young guy always asks, "So you're going to talk all about *Full House*, right?"

So . . . I know I must speak of it because the show and its success are a huge part of what got me to this intersection. You don't know it when it's happening until ratings tell you it's happening. People still come up to me on the street and say, "TGIF," which was the name of the block of ABC family sitcoms that dominated television for so many years. People think the show was always on a Friday night, but the first few years of *Full House*, it was on Tuesdays. Apparently people didn't want to watch TGIT. Sounds wrong, especially for kids. Then again, TGIT might've brought more eighteen-to-forty-year-old males to the party.

And then there was the confusion with the chain of restaurants TGI Fridays, "Thank God It's Fridays." Someone liked that expression so much over the years that they made a movie and then named the restaurants after it. Until I just mentioned it I'd forgotten there was also a movie in 1978, starring Donna Summer, called *Thank God It's Friday*. I didn't see it, as I was usually busy on Friday nights.

I wasn't very religious as a Jewish twenty-one year old, but I did find it funny culturally that the movie had that name. If it had been a giant hit, maybe there wouldn't have been a TGIF. Maybe it would have been called TGIS—"Thank God It's Shabbat"—and the restaurant chain would've started Fridays with a happy-hour all-you-can-eat latke buffet, with Mogen David wine coolers. That would've been enough for us. A'ight, enough of that, apologies once more.

So somehow I got this gift of a job, and one that introduced me to the world of family television—playing the straight guy with two other straight guys on a show about three straight men raising three girls in San Francisco. That's the bi-line of the show.

It's still fascinating to me how I came from this edgy-ish comedy background and then this job came along. But I had always loved situation comedy television and it was the kind of job I always wanted, a primetime network sitcom. It was produced by Tom Miller and Bob Boyett, who had made some of the biggest sitcoms of all time.

There was no decision to be made. I'd been fired off a show in New York on CBS, had a new baby to raise, and now was being offered this big family show, on ABC no less. Cut to: me asking the head of wardrobe, "Does it *have* to be a cardigan sweater?"

The sweet father, Danny Tanner, was the personification of fruitiness. His character had originally been conceived, for the pilot, as a guy who basically loved his kids more than anything. But then I worked with the show's producers to embellish him with some other qualities—his being a hugger and a neurotic compulsive cleaner, kind of in the Felix Unger/*Odd Couple* vein. Hugging people a lot and cleaning 24/7 is . . . well . . . do the math. Whatever it was, it worked.

Over the years, men who would seem physically threatening have sauntered over to me, looked me in the eye, and instead of saying "I fucking hate you," came at me, their eyes welling up with tears, and said: "You were the daddy I never had, Bob." It was then I realized the crossover fans *Full House* had accumulated.

After a group man-hug they'd usually shove me into a sidecar of one of their bikes and sweep me into the caves of Griffith Park, where they'd beat me senseless until I repeated for them like a good sitcom actor does, things like: "When do we start shooting? Should I bring the fondue? Oh, I forgot, I don't have to . . . I *am* the fondue." That would usually be followed by the words, "Ow-ow-ow that's my butthole . . ." And other things like that.

I've never enjoyed fondue. Maybe it's because it's a word that I repeat too much, as well as being a word that's always found its way into sitcom scripts. Like *flan* and the expression *But I digress*.

The words *But I digress* are what you often read in a sitcom script when the writers of a character have nothing better for them to say. I've had to say it a few times on different shows. It's the ultimate drinking game if you're sitting home watching every sitcom of all time. Truth be told, there are only so many ways to core an apple.

Speaking of which, my laptop is heating up again and I won't go into detail but I've just put a potholder mitten over my package. But I digress.

So yes, I'm almost done addressing how and why I was "blessed" to land on *Full House*. *Blessed* is a one-word expression some sketchy nightclub promoters have said to me over the years when I've asked them, "How are you doing tonight?" "I'm blessed, man." And they always seem to say this while there's a crazy situation all around them: one girl is trying to break through the VIP line, another is vomiting on her stilettos, which are now ruined—and they're not even hers because she borrowed them from her roommate, and now the faux-suede fabric is stained forever and they have to be thrown out before she gets in the cab to go home . . .

Scares me that I knew that world for a while. "A while" meaning a couple decades. That was after *Full House* ended and I was going through my stereotypical forty-year-old's midlife crisis, which I'm probably only halfway through. Life itself can occasionally be two-dimensional.

Which brings me back for a moment to Danny Tanner, the admittedly somewhat two-dimensional character I played, on a family sitcom aimed at twelve-year-old girls. People ask me all the time about the character and why I am not like the guy on the show in real life. I've met people who've watched every episode and own the boxed set and can recite all the lines and even know where the music cues came in.

If you're one of those people, bless you. I mean it. I could've used those people while acting on the show, because I never knew my lines or why I was saying them. Not totally true. I knew why I was saying them. To put my kids through college.

I do want to state that the show sometimes tackled significant issues, right in your face, and dealt with them by "talking" about them, as sappy as that may have seemed. *Full House* was actually rooted in healthy family-therapy doctrine. So in some ways the show was three-dimensional, or hell, four-dimensional. If you're the Octomom, eight-dimensional. You know at least five of her kids have watched *Full House*.

But my point is, just like there's a place for a movie like *The Aristocrats*, there's a place for a show like *Full House*. *FH* was meant to be able to be watched by everyone. And it relieved some parents from having to actually bring up with their kids' issues like bullying or drinking at prom. Seeing those subjects covered, however lightly, on *FH* gave them a point of entry. Again, I don't full-on believe in this theory, but it has been told to me . . . a lot. And if you hear something enough, it starts to influence your belief system.

Some people are too cynical these days about anything that is teaching kids good morals. I understand that preachy "family values" are a turnoff for many. But again, there is definitely a place for it. A need for it. A void. Some people still want that feel-good TV show or movie, just the same way the rest of our culture wants good solid chop-people-up zombie TV shows or movies.

Between the chop-people-up zombie TV shows and movies that get made and the reality shows that abort their way onto the air, we do seem to be getting farther and farther away from the purity and intended beauty of what *Full House* was. Something you can actually watch with kids. Even the littlest of kids. Now we are in a world where toddlers just sit there, with or without an adult, watching the nightly news in all its gruesomeness.

Okay, for a second, grant me this one digression on the nightly—hell, the *daily* news . . . You know how when they're about to show you a shooting or a bombing fully captured live on camera, they tell you, before you have a chance to look up from your soup, "What we are about to show you is violent and could be mentally disturbing, especially for children. Okay, now that we've told you, please enjoy this footage of the same murder that you're going to see for three days over and over and never be able to get out of your mind."

That is when I say, "Fucking stop this. Where's Webster when I need him? Gimme *Mr. Belvedere!*" Or just wait and only show that insidious news clip of heinous hell on earth late at night, so little kids won't be awake to see it. It desensitizes them. Becomes part of their emotional lives. Unfortunately not everyone is blessed with parents who can help redirect or navigate them away from the bombardment of negative and horrifying stories and images.

Whew, where did this soapbox come from? Look, some may say I'm a hypocrite to preach about what's suitable for kids. Yes, I'm occasionally on cable late at night doing an R-rated turn of comedy, but I take responsibility for my adolescent rants. If a warped teen watches my stand-up, the most they get out of it are the same things I found funny as a teenager, and still do: penis and bathroom humor. Nobody gets hurt from that. Maybe a rash, but that's treatable. A running theme in my stand-up of late is telling young college kids not to have sex with sea creatures. Or goats. Or a turtle. Correct me if I'm wrong, but aren't I providing a public service?

I love and look forward to doing more "adult work" (sounds like I'm about to start a porn empire) but I also, to this day, cherish shows that may not be geared specifically for kids but do put out good values. And kids can watch them. Like a show I got to be a small part of for many years, the sweet, charming, and full-of-love *How I Met Your Mother*.

That show is about the search for love. Something we all need. I could use some right now in fact. Here I am sitting in bed on a Sunday typing on my laptop like Diane Keaton in *Something's Gotta Give*. Yes, I am a single man sitting in bed, writing something I'm passionate about, living the life of a chick flick. And . . . loving it (*see:* Don Adams in *Get Smart* episodes for correct cadence on that catchphrase).

From an adult (yet made for everyone) show like *How I Met Your Mother* and going all the way back to *Full House*—made for the kids—I've learned figuratively how to be a parent for children other than my own, as creepy as that may sound. It's part of my life's journey. I've put my entire soul into raising my own daughters, and will continue to, because it's the most rewarding part of my life. But they've also inspired me and taught me how to embrace and step up to that honored role of being a father in general. I get college audiences with thousands of people looking at me apparently as the dad they wish they had. And yeah, it's only for an hour, and about as superficial a connection as can exist compared to actual real-life parenting. But I still take it very seriously. That's not the comedian part of me using the word *seriously*.

I've said this before and I think it sums up my warped comedy: I wouldn't hurt a flea. I'd finger a spider though. I remember tweeting that and then having a momentary second thought. But how is a stupid line like that gonna hurt anyone? And if it makes some people laugh, I've done a nice thing.

It's healthy for people to get out of whatever mode they're in and have a meaningless giggle. It's a breath with a smile attached to it. And what spider is gonna be offended by that? They don't even have brains that could comprehend a joke that's intent is to violate them. On that spider-fingering line, one person tweeted back, "Which sets of legs does the spider pull apart for me to finger them?" Those are my people.

And staying on the subject of parenting other people's kids— I'm almost done with this rant by the way—if a kid read that tweet about my wanting to finger a spider and decided to do so . . . yes, I admit, he could hypothetically get bitten by that spider, and I do know a person can die from a spider bite. Therefore, I hope I am not too late with this declaration to kids everywhere: *Do NOT ever finger a spider!* Under any circumstances. You can die.

See, that's parenting. As an actor or a human, I can never go back to it in the *Full House* sense. But I am damn proud I did that show. I have friends now—I know, "good for you, Bob"—who tell me they watch *FH*, including one who's a thirty-to-forty-year-old woman (trying to stay safely nebulous on age), and she says, "It just makes me feel good."

Case closed. It worked. So, for one brief shining TV moment, there was a sweet show that may have been cheesy—but where morals weren't added in an ironic way. The writer and the cast meant that shit. And some of us are better for it.

With the genre of family sitcom, there's always a lesson learned. It's true even with *South Park,* a brilliant show that I'll always revere. They often end an episode with: "And what have we learned today?" The answer may come from Cartman, who says, "It's bad to hate Jews," or "Be nice to people or they'll kill Kenny."

On *Full House,* at the end of the day, no one went to bed angry with each other. You only had twenty minutes; you couldn't. Going to bed angry is reserved for a two-parter. Wish my life was always like that. Maybe as I get older, I am becoming like a lot of people: "Why can't everything just be wrapped up kindly and nicely with a big metaphoric bow around it so I can go to bed more easily?"

Nothing too selfish. Just want to be kind to others, be treated with kindness in return, and get some friggin' sleep. 'Cause at the end of the day, it's the end of the day. And I need some friggin' sleep! Springsteen said it best: "Because the night belongs to lovers." What?

So before I turn away from all this talk about why I will always love and be proud of *Full House* and launch into all the dirt from the show that I know readers are clamoring for, let me first start by acknowledging it's been complicated at times to be so heavily associated with the name Danny Tanner. It's a name I have said and heard uttered more than one would want to imagine.

Oh, Danny Tanner . . . he was a man who was more than a man. He was a widower and he was full of woe. He was a woe-man.

I spent twenty years trying to "opposite day" how some people regarded me. Although if I'd played Steve Urkel I wouldn't have needed to spend the amount of therapy time that got me to here from . . . Danny Tanner. Once you take off the high-wasted pants and suspenders, you can move on with your day.

I've come to terms with it. Danny Tanner, or "DT" as I now call him, because when I hear that name I get the DTs—I shake and recoil as if someone just said "Beetlejuice" three times . . . DT was a guy I am still proud today I got to play. "He doth protest too much," right?

Occasionally during my *FH* days I'd fritz out, wanting to be the edgy guy on the show—but the show wasn't meant to have an edgy guy. Unless you considered Uncle Jesse, played by my brother John Stamos, to be tough around the edges. But how threatened can you really feel by a sweet, handsome Greek guy with a blown-out mullet, even if he is all dressed in black leather? And Jesus, is he a sweet person. As is Dave Coulier. I mean he was *Joey Gladstone*. You can't get sweeter than that. Goofy, silly, whatever. The man and the character are just fuckin' sweet.

Danny, though . . . Danny was as far from tough as you can get. He DustBusted a vacuum cleaner in the opening titles. I tried to butch him up, but any complaints from me and they took me back to the biker cave for a group lesson. Here's the rub—ahh, right here, that's right, don't stop, look me in the eye and say my name . . . I still knew, even back then, and I know it more today, that portraying a good father for hundreds of millions of people is valuable. Portraying a good person who's two-dimensional is valuable. A courtroom-artist sketch of a good person is valuable.

As I was working on this chapter, I was actually *in* San Francisco. I did stand-up there as I have for many years—San Fran is well-known as an awesome town for comedy. So while I was there, on my way to do press, a kind young driver guy who worked for the promoter I was doing my gig for—ironically his name is Joey—picked me up. And after one interview, I said, "Joey, *cut it out* and take me to the *Full House* house." And he did. And I tweeted it.

People were pretty damn appreciative. I just feel bad that I did a drive-by. It's the only kind of drive-by I've done. For the record, I've never passed an ex's house to see what she's up to. Not made that way. I may be a recovering OCD neurotic, but I ain't no creepster. 'Cept I crept on this house. The *Full House* house. I pray the lady who owns it wasn't home. I am not a person stalker, but I have stalked a house.

I also went there once for a shoot with Conan where we reshot the show's opening credits with an Asian gentleman from Chinatown playing the part of Michelle. That was a trip. But it was especially wild to be there this past time since we never actually filmed anything at that house itself. It's just where the producers put a camera one day for an exterior shot.

Anyway, this was an oddly cathartic moment for me. Because of this book I've been "driving by" this part of my life that I've often tried to run from.

Like a lot of actors on TV shows that were popular around the world, I have often heard: "I learned to speak English watching your show." That's a high compliment until you realize what it means . . . young men from China and Russia walking around saying, "You got it, dude."

Still, that's healthier than their learning English from, say, one of my comedy specials, in which case their first words in English would have been "Cock shit fuck." Damn, and if you recall from the very beginning of this book, I was asked to say that out loud on Conan once and I did—but reading it in print, even after I've provided a disclaimer for it, it still doesn't feel right.

Everyone involved in *FH*—with DT, UJ, and UJ—has had parents come up to them and say, "Thank you, that's the only show I could ever watch with my kids." I've said that to people too, about their shows. I've actually given exactly the same compliment to Louis C.K. and Larry David, although to be fair I watched those shows with my daughters after they'd already become young women.

My daughters and I were never a TGIF type of group. More indie film types. *Harold and Maude, The Diving Bell and the Butterfly,* and *Pan's Labyrinth*—that's what my daughters and I would watch together. Okay, and a little *SpongeBob.*

The favorite show my kids grew up with was *South Park.* They were into harder-core comedy. *Family Guy* also played on a loop in the more recent years. My girls also loved *Gossip Girl,* but I felt uncomfortable watching that with them. At least with *Curb Your Enthusiasm*—and now *Louie*—you know you're getting messages geared toward sexual awkwardness from a single adult male's point of view.

As a parent you never know if you should change the channel when your eleven-year-old is about to see your favorite comedy stars have sex. Odd, I was more prudish in that way than you'd expect. With my daughters. Never had a son to see if I'd apply the same guidelines.

I also couldn't watch *Project Runway* with my daughters. Fathers: that's good parenting. Don't watch TV that features hot girls, especially girls who are younger than your daughters, *with* your daughters present. Or with their friends. Especially if your daughters aren't home. Apologies. I just throw in shit like that for the bros I meet out when I'm touring New Jersey. I'll get a high five over a paragraph flourish like that. And then find Purell.

A'ight, back to *FH*. Let me know if you've had enough by pulling on your right ear. On *The Tonight Show* once, Jay Leno summed up *Full House* by saying, "The premise of this show is, Mom's dead—let's party." A lot of people could relate to the tragic premise. One of the most rewarding parts of working on a show like that was hearing from thousands of people who'd lost someone, men who'd lost their wives and had to raise their girls as a single parent.

The show hit close to home for many. Except "real people" didn't talk like that, in that amped-up sitcom style, or have a four-year-old looking at you perplexed with an unusually loud retort of "I don't know!"

The character of Michelle was funny, how when she didn't get her way, she would say one of her hook lines: "Aw nuts!" That was in the script pretty much every week. It was guaranteed laughs. The writers knew the audience would react well to it. Michelle was comedy gold. Some little-kid fans would say to their parents, "Let's watch the Michelle Show."

Here's something I assume all of you know, so here's stating the obvious . . . The character of Michelle was played by my friends Mary-Kate and Ashley Olsen. If anyone doesn't know why two babies play one character on a television show or movie, it's because in this case, the girls started on the show at nine months old—and you don't work one child as an infant due to child labor laws and basic human dignity. I hope I haven't just offended any sweatshop owners.

Ashley and Mary-Kate were adorable. Children loved them. Everyone loved them. I don't allow myself to receive any negative comments ever made about them. I love them. So it made sense to me and always will that they were beloved. There was no secret magic formula. If children adore you, you are: adorable. I hear it even now from young kids. Magic like that just happens sometimes. What happened in this instance, though, had never happened before and I doubt will ever happen again. It was and is a rarified air.

I will talk more about Mary-Kate and Ashley later in this chapter, but for now let me just say, it upsets me when people jump all over them and talk trash. All the kids on that show are not kids anymore, and they're all lovely people. Family to me.

My dear friend for life, Candace Cameron Bure, who played my daughter D. J., was ten years old when the show began. Jodie Sweetin, who played Stephanie, was five years old. Family to me.

And I don't talk badly about family. Okay, that's not entirely true. I don't talk badly about "immediate" family or my former television family. Wait, what am I doing? This is a book. I fuckin' love *everybody*. And I did—and do—love everybody on that show. Even the occasional sketchy guest star. That includes Mickey Rooney and Little Richard. Good golly, Miss Molly.

So "the show"—I'll call it that for a moment—had to find itself, as all shows do. At first it was more about three buddies. That experiment lasted about two episodes. Seemed weird to watch guys trying to hook up and find dates while three little girls were being raised in the house.

So that mojo was snipped early on. Except John Stamos kept Uncle Jesse as hetero as he could. Have mercy. Me, I surrendered to my feminine side. Again, lots of open communication in the form of morality speeches, abundances of hugging, and . . . deep deep cleaning.

I also think the fact that *Full House* was shot on analog video, not on digital videotape, made a significant difference in how the show is read by the viewer's optic nerve. Just seems more present and crisp, which is why three-year-olds discover it now on kid cable and think it's a current program. I know, the hair . . . I'd say no one has that hair on television, except God bless Danny McBride and *Eastbound and Down,* one of my personal favorites of all time.

I've spoken to a lot of sitcom actors over the years who, like me, sometimes felt frustrated acting on a show like that, like they were talking down to the audience. But what I learned, and not too late—even though being a natural complainer and cynic are a couple of my gifts—was that there is value in making a show for kids, with characters who are easy to figure out.

There may never be another show like it in primetime network television again. It was a feel-good show, like serving your family a big greasy meatloaf on a Friday night. It was comfort food. Nowadays if a family eats a big greasy meatloaf on a Friday night, some health-conscious member of that family might try to cock-block it and ask for vegan meatloaf. I've had vegan meatloaf. My biggest note on it is: Take the word *meat* out of the name.

Maybe it would've been interesting to do a manlier version of *FH,* where the dad comes home from a hard day's work, grabs a scotch, and yells to his freeloader brother-in-law/out-of-work stand-up-comic best friend, "What the hell are you guys still doing here? The week's over! I can take care of my *own* kids! Get the fuck out!! It's TGI fuckin' F time!!"

But that's not how it went down. Nor should it have. The creators of *Full House* made sure that my dad character—not unlike those in the movie it was patterned after (without ever copping to it), *Three Men and a Baby*—was missing just enough alpha male that he needed his no-nonsense handsome Greek brother-in-law and his Bullwinkle-toting, Mr. Woodchuck–puppetin' best friend to help him raise his kids.

What other kinds of guys would you want to bring into your house to help your child through their most formative years? I'm shocked social services didn't knock on the door and take the kids away just based on the premise. Wait, I think we did have that element on the show once. Anyone remember?

But it all still made more sense than *Who's the Boss?* To this day I don't understand what Tony Danza was doing in that house. And was she *his* boss, or was *he* the boss, hence the title? It's best if some things remain unknown. Oh wait, I just got it! "*Who's* the boss" meant they didn't know *who* the boss was. Oooohhh . . .

Full House had a weird premise too. But again, it didn't really matter when you had the guaranteed laughs of Jodie Sweetin saying things like "Well, pin a rose on your nose!" I'm not being sarcastic with that comment. At the start, she was amazing to behold, displaying old-school sitcom abilities in the form of a five-year-old.

One of the things that also struck me from the moment I shot the pilot of the show was what a great actress Candace was. Even though she was only nine years old, she and I were often the protagonists who at the end of the day—at the end of the episode—had to hold the house together. And today she has three amazing children herself, which proves it was inherently part of her character as a young woman to nurture people.

My oldest daughter recently reminded me that she was actually jealous of my going to work and having a completely different family.

When the show began, I once said on *Late Night with David Letterman,* that my eldest, who was one-year old at the time, thought I was cheating on her because she smelled my TV baby on me.

I was spending more time in the day with little actresses pretending to be my daughters than with my own daughters.

But I actually did change Mary-Kate's and Ashley's diapers once. And that was four years ago. Ashley came up with the punch line to that joke. No, really, I did have to change them a couple times. Cameras were rolling and one of the young ladies had made a poop, which had to be removed or we would have been holding a child with a smashed-poo-filled diaper for a long scene. A *very* long scene if you're smelling poo the whole time. The smell of poo can make the smallest moments seem like an eternity.

I didn't want the poo to cause a rash and soil my television child's butt, so I decided to take the time to remove the aforementioned substance from the diaper, so that my television baby was poo-free.

All poo aside, a bunch of people have asked me, "Did you know Mary-Kate and Ashley were going to become big television stars and eventually transition into the great impresarios of fashion they have become?" My answer is usually sarcastic, though not meant to be snippy: "Yes, that is exactly what I predicted. I am the Nostradamus of show business."

One cannot project the future of anyone on this earth, even if you see the best things opening up for someone, or sometimes, not the best things. Ashley and Mary-Kate always had a good eye, the left one, and I always felt, once they were eighteen, they could make good decisions for themselves. The life of all young women have their ups and downs.

They were more than aware of the "countdown" that people had conjured up that led to the *day* when they'd both turn eighteen. As if millions of guys would suddenly have their chance to have their way with the twins. What a smarmy group of douchebags.

I felt protective of Mary-Kate and Ashley—and equally so with Candace and Jodie. Same as I do with every child actor I've ever worked with. It's "work" we do together, and yet, they are kids, and I am supposedly representing their dad, a father figure who knows the difference between right and wrong. I was proud to be their "dad." I feel like I've always had a connection with kids. Maybe it's because in some way I'm still that nine-year-old wanting to say the things I'm not supposed to say. And the children I've worked with always liked me, I'm told, because I was still one of them.

I am not an ageist. I don't understand people who look at those younger than them and believe, "Oh, they're the *children*—we're so much older and wiser." I can look at a three-year-old and think she has more knowledge than me. Then again, some three-year-olds do know more than me. When my youngest daughter was born, she looked right through me at her moment of birth. It was that look of "I'm onto you."

I'll always have genuine affection for my dear friends Candace Cameron Bure, Jodie Sweetin, Ashley Olsen, and Mary-Kate Olsen for being such important, genuine friends in my life. And the incredibly sweet Andrea Barber, who played Kimmy Gibbler, the "neighbor girl." I also love dearly Scott Weinger, who played Candace's boyfriend Steve on the show. I didn't remember if he had a last name, but according to IMDB, it was "Hale."

But as brothers in arms go, the strongest relationships I made on that show were with Dave Coulier and John Stamos. I'd known

Dave as my best buddy since I was twenty-one but didn't know John until the shooting of the pilot. With them, I had the good fortune of playing with siblings in silliness. Dave acted like a seven-year-old, which eventually made him the youngest person on the set.

Being silly helped us survive a super-clean-cut show that at first mostly got panned but then in retrospect became part of family-television history. Dave, John, and I would egg each other on and we were often driven to outbursts of non-family-friendly humor. When this happened, the producers and the parents of the kids would take us up to the conference room for a good talkin'-to. Those moments were more memorable for me than some of the episodes. I'm not always the quickest study.

For example, when we would go over the scripts together in a conference room with the producers and writers, we were all supposed to be taking notes but I'd be drawing penises on the scripts and showing them to Dave and John like I was in fifth grade. I couldn't help it. The whole show for me was like a beautiful Jekyll and Hyde experience.

Dave used to look at me and say, "You'd kill yourself if I wasn't here." And then he would fart. Loudly. On cue. The set always smelled like his ass. All the show's eight seasons of outtake gag reels have the whole cast leaving the stage abruptly the moment Dave releases his ass fumes. It gave true meaning to the term *gag reel*. It was his signature. His character's tagline was "Cut it out." And he did. Dave's been saying that line in his stand-up for years. He's a really funny stand-up. And he has quite a talented butthole.

As I mentioned, I've been good friends with Dave since long before we were on the show together. We met in Detroit at an open-mic bar called the Delta Lady when he was seventeen and I was twenty-one. When Dave first moved out to L.A., he stayed on my couch in my one-bedroom apartment in an area of Los Angeles called Palms, and pretty much all he did was make fart jokes in between going out with me to the late-night comedy clubs.

Ironically, that was also the whole premise of *Full House*—that my friend Joey Gladstone stayed with me in my "alcove" because he had no place to live. More than ironic that thirteen years before the pilot of that show, Dave really did live with me. And he was cast on the show a year before I was. If *Full House* had been any more real, that alcove would've had a toilet smack-dab in the middle of it and smelled like shit. As Dave used to say, it should've been called *Out House*.

One of the staple directors of *Full House* was Joel Zwick. I call him a "staple" director because since his days on *Full House,* he has had surgery and his abdomen is held together with staples. Anyway, Joel's wife is a shrink and one day—in about the seventh season of my double doodies of working on *America's Funniest Home Videos* and *Full House*—she told me I was having a "manic episode." I was running around on set, walking on the furniture, without touching the ground, like a little kid does when he pretends he's walking on rocks to keep from falling in the imaginary river around him.

I was just fooling around. My friends, the entire cast of the show, were crowding around me and coaching me to go crazier to make them laugh. It was often like this: they would enjoy saying to me, "Bob, do something physical and pass out."

One time I was holding a cup of coffee, and on their cue, I threw it without thinking, onto a wall of high-voltage lighting switches.

Luckily, no fire started, the coffee mug just fell to the floor, but I was appropriately scolded by producers like a kid in school getting sent to the principal's office. And rightfully so. There were people around.

Unless cameras were rolling, I was pretty much not Danny Tanner. Oftentimes I was in a zone of completely committing to that character. People could relate to him. They had fathers and family members he reminded them of. I used to be more like him. I was raised to be more like him.

I was committed to playing someone who possibly should've been committed himself. For his OCD neurotic qualities. And yes, I drew from some of my own baggage to help him flourish. I was in real life a yuppie-type father with shades of *The Big Bang Theory* over-the-top character traits.

I am a hugger by nature, and lately I've found it's the best way to avoid touching people. If you're hugging them you're usually just touching their clothes, not their skin. I also agree with the Howie Mandel theory of fist-bumping and not clasping someone's hand to welcome them or say good-bye. I just feel like whenever there's a situation with lots of handshaking, everyone is thinking the same thing: Where was that guy's hand before he shook mine?

When a salacious person comes up to you and grabs your hand and doesn't let go for what seems like an eternity, it can be off-putting. "My God, that guy is so greasy and his hands are Shrek-sized, and he won't let go . . ." In a case like that, you may want to bypass the hand sanitizer and go right to amputation.

Interesting the meaningless whiny complaints we come up with as human beings, that in the scheme of things are the size of a tick on a gnat's ass. He opened for me once. Gnats Ass. He was an open-mic-er German comedian.

Okay, one of the weirdest things that I should not share, especially in a book, and especially since I am basically anti-drugs-ish, is this story . . . This is a story that John Phillip Stamos actually told on television. If I was smart I'd let it die post-broadcast, but I think you've gathered by now about where my IQ level is at. Gnats Ass.

Before my friend Craig Ferguson took over *The Late Late Show* on CBS in January of 2005, I guest-hosted the show for one night a month earlier. I was the last of the revolving hosts, and shocking as it may seem, my first guest was John P. Stamos. He had warned me he was going to tell a story that showed how crazy I was while we were making *Full House*. I asked him not to, but as usual, I ended up saying, "Oh, you do whatever you want to do." I love John, so I figured it would be fine.

The story he told on the air was one I am hesitant to share in this book. So hesitant, here it is . . . About six years into *FH*, I was going through a bit of a manic period . . . again. I'd drive off after the show we'd just shot and do stand-up at the clubs in town—Comedy Store, Improv, Laugh Factory.

During that time my family was going through another rough patch. My sister Gay was in the hospital with scleroderma. I'd visit her late at night after having shot the show all day and then go off to do a set of stand-up to let off some steam, then return to Cedars-Sinai hospital to see her.

She was in a bad state and needed some company and love. She had no sense of time, so I didn't feel bad about showing up at the hospital at two A.M., which was when she was sometimes just waking up from the meds. I had a wife and kids at home, but after a day of family-television dialogue, I'd release my demons for a little while onstage and then see my sister, who was going through the toughest time a person can go through.

Anyway, back to the story that I really shouldn't be telling . . . the *Full House* filming that week was a particularly child-friendly episode featuring several little-kid guest actors. I believe it had to do with the character Michelle's birthday. I'd research it, but it's painful enough to recall, so I'm comfortable just winging it. Who really needs facts checked for this story? For the episode, there was going to be a birthday cake with lots of whipped cream. It was some kind of slapstick cute silly bit.

Dave, John, and I were waiting backstage. We had been waiting awhile—they were still busy shooting some scenes of Michelle and her friends—and I was getting impatient. "When are they gonna use us? We've been backstage for an hour." Real whiny-actor low-level-thinking sitcom stuff. Meaning—well, just spoiled and bored. Bitch-boy behavior.

I was going nuts: "Why are they taking so long?" I had no right to complain. Shooting my scenes wasn't any harder than what the kids had to do. And they were kids. My acting on that show was like playing Twister: "Left. Red. Good, Bob, now move to the kitchen door."

But whatever, what happened, happened. Not proud of it—and shouldn't share it. So here it comes . . . I couldn't take it anymore. I grabbed Dave and John and we went into the prop room backstage and locked the door. I believe the same prop room they used on *Friends* years later, when they inherited our stage, but I doubt they ever did this . . . Well, not as a group.

Prop room door double-bolted, I swung open the refrigerator, and behold! Six cans of whipped cream. Reddi-wip. Yes, that's how it's spelled. Nitrous oxide is dangerous. Can cause brain damage. But not in Reddi-wip. There's not enough in there to make a woodpecker fart. Reddi-wip is still my favorite dessert topping. I hope that gets me clearance to mention it.

I think when I tried nitrous oxide once maybe in 1980, in a different form, known as whippits, it gave me an actual buzz. Which is what gave me the lame impetus years later to suggest this act of foolishness. Dave and John followed my lead and we inhaled the little bit of air still left in the cans that were meant for Michelle's birthday cake scene. I guess we got high, don't think so though. It was hard to tell, 'cause we were in a hurry and whipped cream started squirting out quickly.

I was an idiot. Oh my God, what a good caption for my next T-shirt. We were laughing, paranoid to be doing something so dumb. And for those of you thinking you want to try this—it doesn't work. It's stupid. And you don't even get high; you just end up looking like someone had recently pleasured your mouth. And if done to ridiculous excess it can maybe cause irreparable brain damage. So can pleasuring someone's mouth, if they have an infection they haven't told you about and it spreads like a flesh eating virus.

We cleaned up; left the cans as they were, now sans the tiny jolt of nitrous oxide that once propelled their cream; and exited the room—not a moment too soon either, as we were needed on set for the birthday cake scene. We got out there, a little dazed but present. The prop people were trying to prep the cake with extra whipped cream for the bit that was about to take place, but as you'd guess, nothing came out of any of the cans.

The producers were a bit annoyed. You think? Here we were trying to shoot the scene and no whipped cream to be spewed. Our prop people were tops, so they futzed with it and it looked fine. If I do recall at all, one of the prop men, I believe "Property Bob," visited another nearby set and brought back a couple tubs of Cool Whip: the topping that required no nitrous oxide. Less slapstick—less cream to be dispensed.

People ask, so here's the other thing I should not have done while working on that show . . . They gave me a rubber doll to talk to as a stand-in for camera run-throughs to represent the character of Michelle. Maybe you can finish this story for me please.

Ashley and Mary-Kate were in school, so I had to camera-rehearse without any other characters and just the technical crew, with this four-foot-tall rubber doll. Only adults were there. A lot of crew guys whom I liked to make laugh. What could have happened next? Oh yeah, so I'm throwing it around, pretending to do stuff to it, as one would do if there were no child actors within a couple soundstages' distance and you were a comedian with no moral compass in front of a crowd of people . . . and what I didn't know was the television monitors were turned on in the school-room and all the dressing rooms, and in certain offices on the studio lot. Like I said, I was an idiot. Catchphrase!!!

Jodie's mom, Janice, and Candace's mom, Barbara, two very sweet people and great mothers, came down to the stage and said, "Bob, we can see what you're doing on the monitors upstairs!" Jokingly as I could, I said, "Well turn them off, I'm *working* down here!" As usual, they were right. I should have used some part of my rational mind, my parenting mind. But I wanted to make the crew laugh. I wanted to make everyone laugh in a way I wasn't able to do on the show.

What I learned through that experience is, if you're making only a few crew people laugh and you're playing with a life-size doll, and there are no other actors around, *stop it*—take a moment to yourself . . . and call a good therapist.

But all in all, it was a huge amount of fun working on that sitcom for eight years. I appreciate it a lot more now than I did back then. Recently I went back to the Warner Bros. lot to shoot a TV show, and as the golf cart was taking me from stage to stage, I was reminded how different things were when we shot *Full House* on Stage 24.

Security wasn't tough back in 1994 because the world itself was in a different place. One time during lunch, I had the kids from the show in a golf cart and I drove right off the lot onto the sidewalk, out in front of the studios on Olive Avenue in Burbank, and started tooling down the street.

That's pretty much the whole story. We didn't rob a liquor store or anything noteworthy, but that was my way of doing something a bit rebellious and off-road that broke the day up for the kids. To sell books, I should probably add that we ran over a couple security guards in front of the main gate, but it just didn't happen.

Truth is, behind the scenes it was often as sweet and gooey family-wise as it was on the air. Yes, I said and did things that were somewhere in between where I am today with my twisted sense of humor and where I was then with the show. But when all is said and done, it was just Dave, John, and me screwing around, sometimes saying irreverent things, as subliminally as possible, around incredibly talented young people, just to make the work seem more fun. It was a time of silly subliminal immature humor.

Since then, Ashley has told me that she and her sister knew when everyone was laughing at something inappropriate, but they just didn't know what it was. None of the kids did. Until they got older. Regrets, I've had a few, but then again, too few to mention . . .

It's a gift to make children laugh. But for me it's even more fun to make them laugh once they've grown up. Since the show went off the air I've spent the twenty-plus years since hanging out with all my former cast members. Feels weird to write *cast members*— they are my lifelong friends.

In particular, all of them have been supportive of me personally over the years with the benefits I've done for the Scleroderma Research Foundation.

I've also had other TV kids on other sitcoms, people whom I love and who are mostly grown-up now—the incredible Kat Dennings and Brie Larson on a great short-lived show called *Raising Dad,* and the super-talented Jared Kusnitz and G. Hannelius on a shorter-lived show called *Surviving Suburbia.* I'm told I may one day work with kids again because the statute of limitations has run out on all of the restraining orders.

As whacked as I may be as a person sometimes, I take very seriously the responsibility of child actors in general. Most of them didn't even choose to go into this profession, and all of a sudden they're thrown on a set with a lot of people who become their "instant family."

It's a conundrum for actors—some work the rest of their lives, most do not. But to be a child actor is often to be a survivor and go deeper as a person than a lot of people ever have to. Childhood is hard enough, and to throw in that additional component can be complicated.

I treasure the relationships I have had—and will always have—with all my gifted friends whom I had the privilege of getting to know through work, when they were very young humans. They keep me young. I am much more responsible as a man today than I would be without them in my life.

And when little kids somehow find themselves in an audience when I'm performing as a standup—because their parents do not know the tenor of my comedy, I do not swear until they are escorted into the lobby and quickly given a shot of Jack at the bar.

Chapter 7

THE BIPOLAR WORLD OF FAMILY TELEVISION

When it first started, little boys used to call it "the people-who-fall-down show." Men used to call it "the guys-who-get-hit-in-the-nuts show." I thought of it fondly as what TV host Tom Bergeron to this day calls "the annuity." I'm talking of course about *America's Funniest Home Videos,* a blooper show no one had ever seen the likes of before it originally aired. I was fortunate to be invited to become the first host.

For years people have asked me, "Who wrote your jokes on that video show?" And the answer is: I wrote 'em with two Canadian gentlemen. Back then there was an 18 percent exchange rate on humor. One of those two Canadians was Todd Thicke, who still produces and writes the show today for Tom. The other writer was Robert Arnott. He wrote for the Smothers Brothers show and many variety programs throughout the heyday of variety television.

When we were working on *AFHV* together, Arnott had a very

funny saying . . . he told me he was waiting for his "fuck-you money," so he could afford to never have to work again, but the most he'd come up with 'til this point was "Fffff . . ."

Together, he and I and Todd would write fifty-five pages a week, and that includes the wraparound host-y stuff that I was as critical of as my critics. It doesn't really help, but when someone's about to insult your work, I guess there's a sense of relief that you've beaten them to the punch by trashing yourself first.

Another case of retrospect: I am incredibly proud of our work on the show. We also wrote—and I'd record—the voice-overs, where I would do my five different voices of kids falling off of things, animals falling off of things, and pants falling off of people where we'd blur their ass and balls. Today, things don't need much blurring. Just some occasional ass crack or wiener coverage. We have really evolved as a culture.

Daniel Tosh has one of the highest-art versions of the show today, but every clip show is easily trumped by YouTube's on-slaught of intentionally and unintentionally made clips. I can't believe I was at the forefront of the "fall down on tape" movement. I am the self-proclaimed pioneer of pain.

Actually, the man who hired me, Vin Di Bona, we could crown as the Emperor of Anguish. And I don't mean that in a negative way. I was just looking for some alliteration, which was always the key to writing good blooper-show dialogue. Pedantically plodding, pursuing priceless pre-records of people precariously punched in their penises.

What a brilliant lead-in for a tape block of men-getting-hit-in-the-nuts copy! We would just hope we could get it past Broadcast Standards and Practices.

BS & P. Broadcast Standards and Practices. That's the department at a network—whether it's one person at a desk at a cable network or a ten-person division of a major network television company—that tells you what you can and cannot say. I used to try to say things that were "edgy" on the video show, like "Here's a bunch of clips spewing in your face . . ." "Let's thrust forward into this next package." In any case, no one seemed to know or care about my "secret code" of wannabe irreverence.

By the way, I really liked our ABC network's broadcast standards executive. Seriously, she was a kind smart lady who knew we wanted to say *cock and balls* on the air, so she had to research to make sure there weren't any new secret metaphors for *cock and balls* that she didn't know about. That's a hard job for a person with dignity—to have to go out of your way to look for cock and balls.

One time I wanted to say *sheep dip*. Innocuous enough. If I recall, there was some video with sheep in it and I was trying to refer to stepping in their excrement. In the recorded voice-over, I simulated a flock of sheep complaining they were "stepping in sheep dip." In a sheep voice I said, "Look out, Daisy, you're gonna get your pretty feet covered in sheep dip! Bahhhh!!" The BS & P lady had a problem with it. Apparently sheep dip is a real thing, a chemical the sheep is dipped in before being sheared for its wool. She forbade me to say it because of legal concerns.

What that means, I don't know. Maybe farmers would have found it offensive. Or maybe she didn't want to run the risk that a kind farmer might be watching the show with his family and, upon hearing me mention sheep dip in the context of "sheep feces," he'd get up during the commercial break, go to the barn to check on his sheep, suddenly find himself disoriented, and accidentally step in shit, ruin his slippers, and sue the network.

Let's be honest, she was just trying to keep me from implying the word *shit* on the air. Real problems we had. Embarrassing for me to admit today; I took it all very seriously. But I let that one go. You gotta pick your battles. Silly funny discussions over a silly funny simple little blooper show.

In today's world, and on today's incarnation of a home-video-type show, they would not only step in sheep shit but would show it coming directly from the source and then have a dumb farm guy falling facedown in it.

The video show itself was a miracle of television history. And me suddenly becoming the host overnight was another very fortunate moment in my broadcasting career. I was acting on "the House that was Full" and I got a call from my friend and manager Brad telling me this gentleman Vin Di Bona wanted me to host a clip show that was made completely of people's . . . *timpani drumroll* . . . home videos. His producer Steve Paskay had seen me on *The Tonight Show Starring Johnny Carson* narrating my actual wedding video on the air when I was twenty-six.

Steve and Vin thought I seemed like a natural fit to host a show where people would send in their personal tapes of their lives. Good idea. Beginning of YouTube. Changed the world of television. And I got the job. And I thought it was just going to be a one-hour special. What I didn't know was, I'd stepped in sheep dip once again.

They'd sent me a VHS videotape of people falling off of things, getting hit in the nuts, getting married, getting hit in the nuts again; babies talking in full sentences; and animals going insane.

I was immediately drawn to the raw product. The pilot hour aired against a rerun of *60 Minutes* at seven o'clock on a Sunday night, and it beat it in the ratings. The next day we were picked up for thirteen episodes. I was again the star of a show that was meant for "family hour."

The seven P.M. hour on a Sunday meant something special to me because *Walt Disney's Wonderful World of Color* had been on NBC at seven thirty P.M. when I was a kid. And I loved it. And I could watch it with my parents, which is not something most kids wanted to do. Watch TV with *my* parents. My parents were actually so proud when I became the host of the video show, they would've probably gone door-to-door themselves to random families' houses to watch them watching me on it. They were that proud.

When the opportunity arose with *AFHV*, I was all in and committed to it as fully as I could be. I was a lucky bastard. Most of the time, the show was fun to make. And the videos were funny. And people let us into their living rooms, and bedrooms, and bathrooms. Many tapes did not make the air. And I saw some of them and am still damaged to this day. I mean, we *really* got to see inside people's bedrooms and bathrooms—and it wasn't pretty. Sometimes it looked like they had been created by the set decorator from *The Silence of the Lambs.*

The funniest video they couldn't air back in the day was one that everyone all over the world has now seen: The monkey in a tree who scratches his asshole and then sniffs his hand and then falls out of the tree. From the smell of his own asshole.

I wanted to show the clip when I was hosting *Saturday Night Live,* but ABC or the producers of the video show wouldn't allow it to be shown. The reason given was that it was ABC property. Who would want to claim that, right? "No, you cannot have the clip of the monkey scratching his asshole—it's property of ABC." But it finally aired on the show. I saw that as an animal-rights victory. And a victory for anyone who's ever had an itchy asshole.

The most upsetting tapes were those where people really got hurt. I don't do snuff. It's wrong. Although as I've said in my stand-up, it *is* one take and you're outta there. Okay, so a young screener who worked for the show sent to my home a tape of a guy wearing a wetsuit, standing in front of a pool with a rubber trampoline-like cover over it. Sounds ominous and enticing, don't you think? The screener told me, "Watch this, we can't air it on the show, but it was made especially for you, Bob." I put the tape in my VCR. By the way, I just typed *VCR*—that stands for "videocassette recorder." You can buy one online right now for ten dollars, hard cash. Wow.

Another fast detour—one of my early jokes was a palindrome. "*Wow* backward is *wow*. And *wow* upside down is *Mom*. And *Mom* upside down is Dad's favorite thing."

All right, so this guy is yelling directly into the camera, standing with his rubber-covered pool directly in front of him. Okay, maybe it wasn't rubber, but whatever it was made of, it was pulled taut like a trampoline. The gentleman looked a bit like the Wild Man of Borneo, or the Tasmanian Devil, whichever means more to you at this moment. And into camera he yells something like, "Okay, Bob Saget, I got a video for you, and it's gonna be great!!"

And then he climbs up this ladder leaning against a tree, goes up about ten rungs, and yells back to the camera, "Okay, Bob Saget—here I go!!" Or something like that—it was impossible to understand him, because his face was covered with hair and much of it looked to be growing from inside of his mouth as well. It was obvious he was going to attempt to dive onto the pool cover from off the ladder and bounce, daredevil/WWE style.

So I'm watching this at home alone thinking, Okay, he's gonna jump off the ladder and land on the pool cover and perhaps it'll all cave in and he will possibly almost drown—but he'll be okay, because the intern screener who sent it to me wouldn't have sent it if the guy *wasn't* gonna be okay, right?

But suddenly the guy's foot gets caught at the top of the ladder while he's saying, "Watch this, Bob Saget!!" and then he screams and falls off the ladder as it drops out from under him. And the scream is *loud* and the sound of him smashing onto the cement ten feet below is LOUDER. And I'm watching this clip, and it keeps rolling—and he isn't moving. Then it runs for another ten seconds—and still he hasn't moved. After another twenty seconds it slowly fades to black. Without the man ever moving again.

I picked up the phone and called the screener directly: "Man, what the fuck did you send me? That's snuff. Did the guy die? What did you send me?!"

The screener—who was a nice kid—was laughing: "No, Bob, he just broke a few ribs, he's fine."

I told him, "Well next time please put a Post-it on it that says, 'The guy didn't die, he just broke a few ribs.' I can't do snuff, man!"

Another video I can't get out of my mind was also not airable. Two supersized people in a shower having sex. Smashing their parts up hard against the shower door. Laughing and schtupping. It goes on for a little while and then the shower door breaks, and the two naked lovers fall hard onto the bathroom floor, still laughing. Even though at this point they are mostly below the locked-off camera frame, you can still hear them laughing hysterically, flopping around on the floor like two sea manatees. And you know there must have been broken glass on the floor, but they didn't seem to care, just a-laughin' and a-laughin'. They must've really been fucked-up.

Both the shower video and the pool one are really nothing compared to what you see these days, on Daniel Tosh's, Rob Derdyk's shows, and elsewhere. I do wish I could have aired them. Not for the edginess or nudity, but so I could have had the pleasure of announcing, "And the winner is . . . Supersize naked people having sex until the shower door breaks!!!" And so I could have brought them up onstage in body casts with their cuts healing, still giggling as they accepted the check for $10,000.

When hosting *SNL* in 1995, the great comedy writer Al Franken, who is now an esteemed senator from Minnesota, wrote a sketch I helped contribute to. The premise was a wrong-as-could-be parody of an episode of *AFHV*. He had titled it *America's Funniest Hate Videos,* and it was me hosting the show but with all . . . hate videos.

There were "Flaming Klansman!" with Michael McKean, "Skinhead Hitting Another Skinhead in the Testicles with a Baseball Bat!" with Mark McKinney and Jay Mohr, and "Headless Militiaman" with the great Chris Farley and David Spade. It was refreshing to be able to make fun of myself and that form in a subversive way with those incredibly talented comedy people.

An *America's Funniest Home Videos* was something that doesn't happen very often. It was an immediate hit. I remember clearly when Vin Di Bona called me on a Monday to tell me we were the number one show on television the night before. It was a cool moment. I appreciated the success I had from the show for its eight-year run with me at the helm.

If I'd have been paid per nut hit I'd have bought an island. Or two. One for each of the two billion nuts hit. If you laid all the nut hits end to end, nut to nut on the ground . . . you could cover the state of Nevada with a very long paper-doll-like daisy chain of men all attached by their nuts. May sound like an absurd premise, but if we could do it, I really believe it could create some national healing. Healing for all those nuts that had been bashed and pounded and winged during the making of the show.

Today, Tom Bergeron does a wonderful job leading the series into its twenty-fifth year on television. The show will live forever. Unlike many of the people in the videos, whom we see falling hard onto the cement until the camera quickly cuts away to a studio member throwing his head back in laughter.

Those two family shows—*Full House* and *America's Funniest Home Videos*—that burst me onto TV ran simultaneously for about a six-year crossover period. I was lucky as hell. Two shows on the air at the same time. Other comedians I'd known over the years used to force me to apologize for taking one of their shows away from them. I was a bit of a maniac from the pace—acting on *Full House* and cowriting the video show and recording all the voice-overs. Regardless, it's the complaint of a complete pussy if he's telling you how hard he has to work each week on a family sitcom while simultaneously hosting and voice'ing-over a video show.

With the voice-over work, I just attempted to copy the great Mel Blanc, the genius who voiced all the Warner Bros. cartoons, including Bugs Bunny and Daffy Duck. Except I had one-hundredth of his range. My dog voice was the same as my little-kid voice. And most of my female voices were just different ranges of my mother's voice. It would've been a good day job for Norman Bates, Anthony Perkins' character in *Psycho*.

A'ight, one last confessional. I did something at a taping of *AFHV* that I *still* feel bad about. I was having a frustrating day. I know, over a blooper show. Anyway, I remember I was wearing a wireless microphone that day, and as I walked to the men's room to take a pee break, I made a gesture to the sound guy, telling him to cut my mic off.

I was standing at the urinal when a crewmember came in to pee next to me, and I jokingly told the guy, "Bad fucking audience today, right? What the fuck's wrong with them?" He agreed, and we had a long pee-filled two minutes of audience bashing. Lotta coffee.

Life lesson learned here: First, don't talk bad about anybody—good luck with that. Second, don't ever leave anywhere wearing a wireless microphone and then speak to anyone. I came back into the studio and said, "How are you guys doing?" A young girl in the stands looked at me innocently and said, "We could hear you in there." It was like a moment from a *Naked Gun* movie.

Turns out the sound guy turned off the house speakers but the audience monitors were still on. I tried to dog-paddle out of it— "Oh, that? The sound guy was supposed to turn the sound off. I always say that about the audience. That's how the crew and I joke around about how *great* an audience is. It's like an opposite-day kind of joke." I still want to apologize to that girl, her family, and the whole audience. Okay, *blanket apology* to all the audiences who came to a live taping of that show.

Another life lesson learned. After eight seasons, and no more mic'd bathroom rants, my time on the video show was winding down. Also my marriage had begun to unravel and this was happening at the same time that my second sister was dying. And as we all know, especially during times of crisis, our personal lives can't help but bleed into our work lives.

When I reflect on those days of making the two family shows, my only regret is that I didn't relax and enjoy it more. Take it easier. It's just family television, not harnessing solar energy. I tried to treat everyone I worked with well. Sometimes I was a bit too serious about the whole thing.

Throughout my work life I've learned that most people are just trying to do their best. And the ones who aren't don't stick around too long—unless they are sleeping with the producer. I was always wide awake. Sleeping is an issue.

Chapter 8

THINGS I SHOULDN'T HAVE DONE

"Things I Shouldn't Have Done." Could be one of the many titles of this book. Some of the things involve my own foibles: neurosis, self-involvement, experimenting with controlled substances in my twenties, and dating people who may have been considered inappropriate for me in my eighties. Sorry, flashed forward.

I feel bad about having done anything that ever hurt anyone. But as long as we learn from our mistakes we don't have to relive them. "Mistakes, I've made a few. But then again, too few to mention . . . I did what I had to do and saw it through, without exemption." For those of you who may not know (hopefully not too many), those are the lyrics to the classic song "My Way," written by Paul Anka and sung by Frank Sinatra. I love that the word *exemption* is in a song. And it's not about taxes.

Things I shouldn't have done. All of us could probably write that at the top of a memo pad and make a list of things we'd like to set the clock back on.

Infidelity. Before I knew what the word meant I thought it was a type of banking. It is actually. If you are practicing infidelity you will wind up being very involved in banking. You will end up going to a bank and withdrawing more than half your account to give to the person you practiced your infidelity upon.

I always wondered, if Fidel Castro cheated on his wife, would the person he cheated with be an "in-Fidel"? Because they had been "in" "Fidel." Thanks, Bob, for spelling that out. Okay, I never wondered that.

I did once wonder if Fidel Castro would've been good playing Tevye in *Fiddler on the Roof*. *Fidel on the Roof* could've worked. Castro was already a dead ringer for Tevye, and it would've been such a happier ending because he could've become the dictator of the village of Anatevka, and no one would've had to flee. A feel-good ending.

We need feel-good things. Life can be really hard sometimes. But it's better than being a butterfly where you only live a month. I posted that statement on the beloved Twitter and one girl answered, "Yes, but that'd be worth it cause it'd be the best month *ever*." I don't think she got the idea: that one month *is* your life. One month and done. Or perhaps she did understand and just didn't care about her life that much.

I can understand that heaviness. Or shallowness. She may just live to party for one month and not care about anything else. I can't do that anymore; I'd retain too much fluid. I don't like to not get stuff done and, on top of that, do harm to myself, possibly others—and on top of *that*, and most importantly, be bloated.

I've taken Midol before. My daughters find that hilarious. I'm concerned it makes me one of them. What's wrong with that? To continue my own discourse, there *is* something wrong with that, because I do not want to be one of my own daughters. Although if I was, I could borrow some of their clothes as sisters do. What?

The Midol thing was—I had a headache and cramps and there were no other pain relievers with caffeine in the house. Too. Much. Information. But I think that's what a book's supposed to be. Well, this one apparently is.

Okay, I'm of course skirting the subject of "things I shouldn't have done." Here goes. I did a bunch of stuff when I was young that I regret. I mentioned earlier how I lied throughout my childhood. I shoplifted meaningless things—toy guns, candy, just crap. Set some fires too. Not like warehouses or mountainsides, but things like sticks and leaves. Little boys do really dumb things. Really good to not do that. And imperative not to do it when you're older.

I've talked to a lot of friends who've told me they too had a weird fascination with fire. At any age a fire starter is an arsonist. How do I come up with these gems? I was really dumb. Here's an example of one dumb thing I did, and with no motivation. That's the worst, when you do something you know is ethically wrong on every level yet you have no motivation . . .

My grandmother, the one we called Bubbe, was visiting us from Philadelphia. I was about nine years old. She was taking a nap in my bedroom, a small room, the middle one upstairs between my sisters' rooms in our sweet little house in Norfolk, Virginia.

I don't know why I did this, but I was with a friend of mine, I think either my neighbor buddy Trey or my best pal, Jonathan—I actually can't remember. In any case, I know I had an innocent accomplice, as this stupid event of foolishness was all my concept. In my room, with my bubbe sleeping, I took an aluminum Band-

Aid box, stuffed it with cotton, poured lighter fluid on it, struck a match, and set it on fire.

I heard my mom walking by and didn't want her to see it, or wake my grandmother, so I quickly slid the thing under the bed. Just like a kid, I now go right to a disclaimer: "It wasn't a high flame." My mom peered her head in and asked me, "What are you doing, Bobby?" I said what all kids say: "Nothing."

She didn't scold me, just walked by and said, "Don't wake Bubbe." After she was out of sight, I quickly took the Band-Aid box from under the bed and blew it out. But somehow that movement and the smell of the extinguished fumes woke my grandmother. Reminiscent of the "Bobby, stop shaking my bed" incident from six years later. Wow, I just realized why my bubbe was already paranoid years later thinking that I was messing with her bed during that 1971 earthquake.

No harm came to my grandmother, the bed, or me, but my mom finally smelled the fumes and then my grandmother told her what I'd done. Bubbe didn't make a big deal of it though. That's why I loved my dad's mom so much. She'd had five sons and knew that sometimes boys do dumb stuff. In retrospect I may have done it *because* I wouldn't get in trouble around my bubbe.

She lived another eight years; no more fires threatened her, just life. The loss of three of her sons and a lot of heartache. Good times too. Lots of laughs. I mentioned earlier the state she was in at the convalescent home in Philadelphia at the end of her life—having suffered a severe stroke—and how I'd take my guitar and serenade her with songs in the hopes to distract and ease her pain.

From the sense memory of those last moments with her it still dawns on me that even today, my four-chord guitar playing and singing could have a euthanasic effect on people. I'm just glad no one has ever brought me onstage and introduced me as "the Claus von Bülow of music." I meant well and deeply cherished my last times spent with my kind father's sweet mother.

Okay, here's a phase I wish I could've bypassed entirely, but I was a teenage boy and I could not avoid my innocuous version of teen perversion . . . Yes, I'm segueing from talking about my grandmother and her passing to delving into a tale about masturbation. If only I'd had a girlfriend when I was the horny teenager I was at fifteen, I could bypass this entry. I would've never bypassed any entry if one had only presented itself. It was hard out there for a wannabe pimp.

As I got to hit my teens, I'd secretly buy *Playboys* at the newsstand and stuff them in my pants with my belt tightened supertight so the mags wouldn't fall down my pant legs and reveal my stash. I came home late one night to my parents' apartment and they asked me to come into their room. Straight-backed, with a magazine-loaded front, I reluctantly entered, fifteen years old and walking like I had a spinal issue.

I had one modus operandi: Must keep the magazines from hitting the ground. I suppose I was age appropriate to be on foot, walking half a mile to the corner magazine stand to buy *Playboys* and smuggle them into my parents' apartment. And again, in my defense, there was no Internet. A prepubescent man's gotta do what a prepubescent man's gotta do. And I'd been a horny little bastard since I was six years old. I think all that came out of me back then was air.

At about eight years old, at my Uncle Sammy's house, I discovered *Playboy* magazines. I always had a thing for "not the articles" but the pictures. That thing is called my penis. And it was more than that. It was my testicles too.

The magazine used to have staples that held it together. Years later, *Playboy* saved many a teenage boy's life by finally becoming staple-less. *Playboy* is bound with glue now. I'm not speaking metaphorically. I mean it's literally bound with glue—before people read it. Nothing sharp to snag any genitalia on. During my obsessive ten-year sexual awakening, in my lonely hours I could've easily positioned the mag incorrectly and accidentally poked a staple into my sac and bled to death.

Just a few years back when I was featured in *Playboy*, rather than go straight to the article about me, like the man-cub I inherently am, I skipped right to the pictures. Semi-man-cub silent pantomime fist-bumps all around.

Other than the soft-core porn, I guess I was relatively innocent as a kid. I didn't do drugs as a "yute." I'd moved so much I didn't even have enough time to meet the harder-core people. And they certainly wouldn't have accepted a nerdy kid like me, or taken me under their wing and allowed me to get fucked-up with them. Well, maybe they would have in a "let's get the dog high" kind of way.

So even though I was age-appropriate as a teenager and resorted to some lying and pilferage, the truth is I was just a nerdy kid who was scared of fucking up and getting in trouble with his mother. I have since come to terms with that issue. Don't you agree, Mom?

The thing about being a teenager is that the difference between right and wrong is often an in-the-moment judgment call. Unfortunately, I've known a lot of people who never learned right from wrong. Many are extremely successful in the legal profession.

It's hard when you're still a teenager—but it's essential to figure out for yourself what you believe in, what's right and wrong. That's why certain "rules to live by," like, say, the Ten Commandments, are maybe more than just a tedious set of dogma. I mean, no matter what you believe in as a human being, "Thou shalt not kill" seems like a perfectly good standard to live by.

And yes, there are always exceptions. "Thou shalt not kill" while "coveting thy neighbor's wife." Doubly wrong. This is why I don't talk religion and politics. I always feel like I'm arguing with myself. And I live alone but once a fight with myself escalates it can really disturb the neighborhood. The only thing that calms me down in that case now is Taylor Swift music blasting through every speaker in my house. Two A.M. blasting from the jacuzzi—"WE ARE NEVER EVER EVER GETTING BACK TOGETHER!!"

So no, I was not a hard-core youth, but I had to learn right from wrong like everyone else. And now, as a proud father of three who is inspired by young people, I sometimes feel like the stereotypical righteous parent telling the teenagers to "just say no"—unless it's really good shit. That's said facetiously, of course. Such a drag to have to add disclaimers, but I also don't want to promote drugs— unless I'm selling them. Shit, did it again.

I just want to be your entertainer, not your gateway to stronger stuff. There's another lovely quote. And don't stick firecrackers up your ass on July 4. You'll be left with a burned-out asshole. If you have more than one asshole you can ignore this because you're one of the fortunate freaks who have an asshole to spare. One can never have too many assholes.

Back to "things I shouldn't have done." Okay, this is a big one. It's about drinking to excess. This isn't a twelve-step book by any means—that's my next one. That will also be a twelve *page* book. Some of the people I have the most respect for are my friends and loved ones who've come out the other side: my twelve-step friends who fought the fight and continue to fight. They have inspired and influenced me to clean up my own act over the years. Not my stand-up. No one can clean that up.

I fantasize that my stand-up specials *have* been cleaned up when they've run in other countries, translated into other languages. I have this feeling people from other lands who speak no English do not even bother to translate my words, so there are no curse words or dirty subject matter. They translate everything I said originally into beautifully clean stories of love and kindness.

But getting back to the drinking I shouldn't have done . . . here's the scene. When I got divorced I was forty-two. *The Hitchhiker's Guide to the Galaxy* said the secret to life is forty-two. It's the answer to "life, the universe, and everything." Kind of stuck with me after I made it through forty-two. To be honest, I was a bit out of my mind then. Damn, I've added that disclaimer to every year I've talked about.

This time it was in 1998. I'd just finished directing the movie *Dirty Work* for MGM with Norm MacDonald and Artie Lange. I came back to Los Angeles from Toronto and returned to live by myself at the beach for a year.

I was creatively inspired but personally adrift. My rewards in life were—and still are—my daughters. When I wasn't out of town working, they lived with me on weekends, so during the week days alone in Los Angeles, I was a newly single man. I tried out the "just divorced shallow older single guy" landscape for a while. A couple years. Okay a little longer, because there was definitely a significant relationship in between a few times over a ten-year period. Until . . . possibly now? Whatever, my drunken "club years" were way too long. And they are over.

I was a fool. One of those idiots who brags to people, while intoxicated, that he can drive better when he's drunk. I repeatedly committed a sin against humanity: drinking and driving. So many young dudes I see out in the world are competitive and wanna buy me shots and say they got fucked up with me. Sorry, bros, can't no more. Shouldn't have then. Can't drink and drive. We lose too many people to it. So with all due respect, forgive my buzzkill fatherly honest advice—but just don't fucking drink and drive.

I'm sorry to preach. I think I preach more to guys than girls because I never had a son. Well, the decade's not over yet. [*Sound effects: record screech*] Fact is, I am lucky to be alive. I have zero tolerance for drinking and driving now—unless I'm driving a public bus.

That doesn't even make sense. I don't think the Los Angeles County Metropolitan Transportation Authority would let me drive one of their public buses even if it was for some television show. Hold on . . . That right there is a great idea we could sell together using the Kickstarter model. Let's all go in as partners on a TV show called *Celebrity Bus Drivers*.

How cool would that be? We could all be "partners" and we would barely have to advertise it because the ads would be plastered on the side of the very same public buses! And the same celebrity bus driver could actually be plastered along the sides and back of the very bus he's driving. Oh my God!! And the celebrity driver could be *plastered* too!! And that is how people come up with marketing ideas that go nowhere. That's right, you're welcome.

I'm now almost emotionally ready to tell you one of the life-changing stories that wouldn't have taken place if in fact I had been on a bus. I am not by any means proud to tell this story, and if I could set the clock back on this one, I'd rewrite, reedit, recast, and relive it.

I was driving back from a college bar in Westwood with a co-median buddy of mine. That was a difficult sentence just now to pinch out. Some of us unfortunately go through a phase like this for some reason. It's a handicap for being mortal in this fucked-up society. Again, no judgment—I mean, I'm calling *myself* out on this one.

As a parent, I look back at my behavior during this time in my life and find it repellent. Okay, some fun times with buddies were had, but looking back, I was a cliché. A divorced guy wanting to do anything but deal with his own life. I was a good father and good at my work, but frankly, how good can you be at anything if you're driving the streets on booze? Not good. So I was fooling myself.

To smack myself around for your reading pleasure, here's how I'd profile myself: I was divorced, dumb, sometimes drunk, and the luckiest asshole in the world for not doing anything that wound up hurting anyone. You may want to get a nice cup of herbal tea and a blanket to get all comfy for this one . . .

The year was 1927—oh, sorry, I fantasized we had just come into "talkies." No, it was not that long ago—well, depending on your relationship with time. Okay, it was 2003, I believe. I was driving home on Sunset Boulevard from the UCLA area heading west to go toward the beach where I was living.

My buddy, a smart, dear, and brilliant comedian friend, was passed out next to me. He will remain nameless because since then he has had plastic surgery and changed his name and moved to

Ecuador. Actually, no, he is very clean and sober and doing great in every aspect of his life. In fact, he has a groundbreaking podcast that I did an episode of not long ago.

So, kids, back to story time—I was driving and I blacked out and drove up the right curve on Sunset Boulevard just east of the 405 freeway. At that instant, my buddy woke up and said, "Man, did you just black out and roll up the curb?" We were actually balanced only on our left wheels for a couple seconds. I quickly slowed down and pulled over to the side of the road and stopped the car and said, "Yes, holy fuck, I could've flipped us."

I was lucky. We were lucky. Again, they say luck is when opportunity and preparedness meet. Not in this case. This type of luck was whatever version of an "angel's blessing" you subscribe to, even if you have no belief system. There was no preparedness involved. And definitely not an opportunity. Except one to change behavior.

I got myself as together as I could, focused on the road, and drove home very slowly, doing everything I could to stay awake. Would never do that now. We all need to pull over and call a cab. Although many of the cab drivers I've called have been more fucked-up than me. Then again, driving a cab is not always a dream gig. I am a master at stating the obvious.

Not long after that night where the dangerous reality of drinking and driving finally sank in for me, my friend worked on himself to clean up. Today, he hasn't had a drink for over ten years. I have, but again, only when I drive the senior citizen mini-van from the Jewish Community Center to the Farmer's Market.

My friend and I did have some fun during our dark times, which makes our reconnecting this past year all the more sweet. Neither of us wants to return to that drunken sea of late-night bickering with young girls who shouldn't be where we shouldn't be. Fuck, I probably just killed my chances of a great booze sponsor for my next tour. But there's always Australia.

When you're out late at a bar, and especially when you drink and drive, it doesn't end up well. Occasionally at the end of the tunnel is a cop just waiting to take you in. A cop took me in once. Into his car, and I had to let him have his way with me so I didn't have to take the Breathalyzer. Another officer actually painted his penis to look like a Breathalyzer to fake me out. He told me I had 5 percent. Just the tip. For clarity, everything after the word *cop* did not happen. When you look up the word *why* you may find this paragraph.

One of the most dramatic driving-after-one-drink escapades I ever went on was when my youngest child couldn't get to sleep with her bunny, her favorite sleep doll. It was a stuffed bunny that had been left behind at her mother's house. So my intention was a good one: get my baby her bunny.

The backstory on the bunny: The stuffing had come out, so one day, like a good newly single father in a panic to calm his four-year-old down, I sewed into it some crumpled paper to give it the appearance of a still-stuffed bunny. I think it was loose-leaf paper. Least that gets softer with time than copying paper.

My daughter asked me, "Why is my bunny so crinkly and hard?" I explained that I'd put paper in it because I didn't know what else to stuff it with at the time—and I'd sewn it up all nice and neat so it wouldn't come out. I'd have been more resourceful if I'd used dryer lint.

When a couple splits up, their kids' things always get mixed between the parents' houses. It can be traumatic, especially if it's something that means a lot to your child. If my parents had ever split up, my treasured item would've been the calf liver I kept in a jar by my bed until I was sixteen. TMI.

So one night my daughter's paper-stuffed bunny was at her mom's house about a half an hour away. I'd had that drink at home—but last-minute, my daughter realized she didn't have her bunny. And she needed it. I didn't want her to be bunny-less for the night, but I think I overreacted a little. To the point where I was mirroring Liam Neeson's character in *Taken:* "I don't care what I have to go through or who I have to go through, but I. Will. Get. My. Daughter. Her. Bunny." I got in my car and zoomed down the Pacific Coast Highway to go to her mom's house to: Get. The. Bunny.

I was stopped by a police officer, who looked me in the eye and said, "Bob, you're going twenty miles over the speed limit. Have you been drinking?" I'll never forget this officer because he was so kind to me. I told him the truth: that I'd had one drink and needed to get my daughter's bunny from my ex-wife's house.

He told me in no uncertain terms, "I could run you to the station right now, especially if you tested too high with an alcohol level. But I'm going to let you go get the bunny if you promise me I won't see you again speeding on PCH, especially with any alcohol in you. Next time I see you I'll take you in, and they'll read about that in the paper tomorrow."

That was a fortunate moment for me. We have all seen those mug shots of people with any fame whatsoever who are taken into the station drunk and end up with a photo for posterity. And it's always either with slicked-back wet hair or hair sticking out in every direction like Doc in *Back to the Future.*

I thanked the officer effusively and slowly pulled out from the shoulder of the road. He followed me, on my tail all the way as I drove the half an hour to my old house. Then he waited around the block as I got the bunny and even escorted me for the entire ride back. That was a very sobering moment.

To this day, I am appreciative of his compassion. The crinkly bunny was finally put quietly in my daughter's bed, and I wrapped her sound-asleep arm around it. Mission safely accomplished. My record was still untarnished and most importantly . . . I got the bunny.

None of my fool stories end this easily resolved. One week later I was driving again on PCH at dusk, rushing to come home from work, and I was speeding again. Completely sober, but speeding. I saw the flashing lights and knew I was getting pulled over once again. Malibu is not that big a community. It was the *same cop*— rolling his eyes, trying to decide if he should just take me in or not. He told me he'd had a bad day and wanted to get home to his family:

"Bob, I told you I didn't want to see you again, and now it's just a week ago that I pulled you over. What do you want me to do?"

"Well, sir, perhaps give me one more chance, and I'll drive slowly and be more cognizant than I ever have in my whole life." It's a book; I doubt I used the word *cognizant.*

He stared me down: "One more time, Bob; you see me again, and I'm taking you in."

I know some of you may think he should've taken me in and I should've paid for my offenses. I said a couple Hail Marys—and I'm Jewish; the closest I'd come before was Bloody Marys. But all I felt was gratitude. Two times he let me off. After that I never saw him again. If I ever do see him again, and it's not under circumstances like speeding on PCH, I'll ask him if he'd like to go for a drink when he gets off work to thank him for sparing my ass.

And then, as we leave the bar, I'll tailgate him and follow him to *his* house and . . . make sure *he* gets home safe. No, you know that's not what I'd do. Maybe I'd just buy him a few shots, drive him back to my place, and let him stay till he was sober. Then we could become best friends and I could invite Dave Coulier over and we would play *Full House* into the wee hours of the morning. And Dave could keep him laughing all night by showing how amazingly he can fart on cue.

I will always be indebted to that officer. I learned my lesson—and I got to get home to my young daughters. Point is, there are some amazing police officers out there and this gentleman gave me just a hand-slap. I could see in his eyes he wanted to do more—like tie me up and spank me.

It just dawned on me that writing that story in this book may not serve my best interests next time I am stopped by a police officer. I'm calling my agents and offering myself up to host as many benefits as the Los Angeles Police Department would like me to do. And if that kind officer happens to be there, I will ask him for the first dance.

That was the end of my reckless drunk-driving period. Definitely the end of it when my kids were at home. Shame on me for my thoughtlessness. Today I am intolerant of drunk drivers. We have all been touched by drunk drivers and the loss of human life due to their recklessness. These days when I see a drunk person weaving down Sunset Boulevard I'll sometimes call 911. I've turned into the safe old-man driver I used to be annoyed at.

Nowadays, if I'm feeling too incompetent to drive, for whatever reason, I just give the wheel up. I mean I literally give the wheel up. I let go of it—and then I play chicken with the drunken white-trash guys in *Dukes of Hazzard* monster trucks. I also enjoy dragging with the small men in black onesie jumpsuits on those motorcycles with the gigantic round rubber tires that go one hundred miles per hour like they're on the autobahn.

No, just the opposite. Every time I get behind the wheel now I take a deep breath and concentrate. Had a multitasking cell-texting problem for an instant when the iPhone first came out, but it didn't take long to come to my senses. Siri has become one of my best relationships.

That's my other road-rage problem with people—texting and driving. People: Stop it. I'll call 911 on your ass. Citizen's arrest. Anyone actually ever done that? Not in today's world, right? Can you imagine that? "Excuse me, sir, I saw you texting and driving—here is my driver's license that proves I am a citizen. I am hereby taking you into custody, in the form of a citizen's arrest. Come on, let's go, pal." [*Sound effects: gunshot*]

I know how lucky I've been. My friend Sam Kinison wasn't so lucky. After all his renegade years he lost his life, driving sober, when he was hit head-on on Route 95 by a drunk driver. Life can be ironic.

Takes me back to a handwriting expert who told me once on air on *The CBS Morning Program* in 1987 that I was "destined to always make the same mistakes." She was incorrect. I won't make that drunk-driving one ever again. I've learned to "surrender the keys" if I need to.

I'll make other mistakes for sure. One of the things I love about getting older is learning from my mistakes. Okay, that's the *only* thing I love about getting older. Although I do enjoy slightly saggy flappy body parts that sound like light applause when I walk.

Here's something else I shouldn't have done . . . It was a long time ago, long before I had any saggy body parts. Little kids play doctor. Some kids play strip club. I was eight years old and living in Norfolk, Virginia, when I did this. A bunch of us kids went into the garage in the house next door to mine. A couple boys and a couple girls. I had a crush on the six-year-old girl who lived there. Again, I was only eight. There were no adults around. Before I tell this story, my advice is, if you are a parent and a bunch of little boys and girls go into the garage, get them outta there and put 'em in the backyard. Nothing good happens in the garage.

Somehow an arrangement had been made—by my next-door neighbor-boy pre-agent type at the time. Again, I was eight years old. The deal was that this young girl next door would show me her private area if I gave her my troll doll. *Troll doll* is not a metaphor, it was one of those little plastic dolls. You know, the ones with the gnomish faces and the hair that sticks straight up. I was eight. Nobody had told me otherwise yet so I thought this was what it looked like down there.

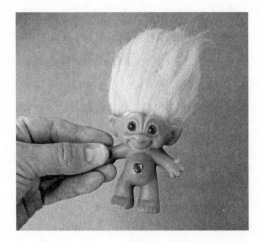

A few kids gathered around, I took out the troll doll, and the neighbor girl took down her pants. And that was that. But somehow it didn't feel like an even trade-off. I actually got scared because I knew somehow it was not the right thing to do—I knew that girls were supposed to wear clothes. But ever since I can remember, I was always trying to look up their dresses. I was a dirty little bastard. Yes, I have grown exponentially.

So I kind of looked at her but panicked and did some dumb-ass little-boy thing like yelling, "Eww." She was a determined negotiator, pulled up her pants quickly, and asked for the doll in exchange for showing me her stuff. I was about to hand it over but then I pulled a little douchebag move. I remember feeling disappointed that there wasn't more to it . . . that was it? I was giving up my troll doll for *that*? It just didn't feel like a fair trade.

Recalling this whole story now, as an adult, validates what assholes men can be and why women are so pissed. You don't make a deal and then back out. How shitty a boy I was at eight to do that. To this day I feel bad enough to vent about it. We'd made a deal and I didn't honor my part in the deal. I wish for her that in her present life, if she has to expose her privates, say, to her husband or to her strip-club-owner boyfriend, that she is treated with respect and appreciation for exposing herself to her man. Or to her woman. Or to the community.

Hers was the first female private area I had ever seen. That I could recall. One that wasn't my point of view during birth. I barely remember the six-year-old girl, so I pray she has no recollection of it. If she does upon reading this . . . it's possible none of that happened.

Despite my blasé reaction, I was actually pretty obsessed at that age with girls' anatomies. I guess I came from a fairly sexually repressed family. Hey, it's better than coming from an overly sexually advanced family. Great argument. In any case, whenever the words *sexual* and *family* are in the same sentence, a therapist should be on speed-dial.

Unbelievably, it's been half a century since the troll-doll episode and I've spent much of those years working on trying to be a better person. Too many guys have no conscience at all. Our culture nurtures that—it prizes he who makes a lot of money and takes advantage of women. But enough about my travel agent's profile on me.

Now, for a moment, I'd like to give you a glimpse into yet another foolish thing I wish I hadn't done back in my struggling-comedian days—1979, when Dave Coulier and I were both living in L.A. As I mentioned earlier, there's an odd synchronicity to the fact that eight years later he and I would be cast together on *Full House*.

I was twenty-three. Dave was nineteen. We did dumb shit. Dumb shit guys do. Some of it was fun. And some of it we shouldn't have done. Here's a harmless but pathetic example . . .

Dave called me from his single apartment in Westwood, at my single apartment in Palms. He was amped up—"Bob, you gotta get over here. There's a bum jerking off in my alley behind a Dumpster!"

Back then I didn't have a lot of excitement in my life. I was just doing spots at clubs around L.A. and staying up all night with other comics—so this seemed like an exciting moment in my day. "Dave, are you serious?! I'll be right there!!"

I jumped in my Oldsmobile Cutlass—gold with a black vinyl

top, with a newly installed cassette deck—and raced over to Dave's apartment. All I recall is double-parking, running into his building, and pounding on his front door. He opened the door and told me with the most depressed look on his face, "He left. You *missed* him." I recall my total loser reaction as if it were yesterday: "*Fuck!* Are you serious?!? He's gone? Where was he?"

Dave took me to the window and said, "He was right out there by that Dumpster, jerking off. I must've watched him for fifteen minutes." I was crushed. What a horrible letdown to such a buildup. I asked him, "Wait, you *watched* him for fifteen minutes?"

Did that mean Dave was gay? And did it matter if he was? And was I gay for going over there to watch a bum jerk off? And did it matter if I was? It was a jerking-off-homeless-man-driven gay-panic moment. Nowadays a guy jerking off in an alley is someone's screen saver. But before the Internet this was the kind of dumb shit we had to do to find our devious entertainment . . . drive across town at sixty miles per hour.

I love Dave like a brother. That's why I can share a story as pitiful as this with his permission. Dave and I had a good time back then. Not many people in my life have made me laugh as much as him. He's one of those solid good friends who will do anything to make you laugh . . . pants dropping, hand farts, mooning cars, real farts, ball sac pulled up over his wiener. [*Sound effects: car screech*]

He's a grown man now, so he had to change his repertoire. He no longer moons people. Unless you're in a restaurant and you ask him to. Dave is a man with a big heart and huge farts. One of my favorite people and one of the most refreshingly immature relationships in my life.

Some of the other things I shouldn't have done—I know you will be shocked—involve John Stamos. Such a great friend. And such an amazing human being. I have so many good stories about him. Most of them involve mirrors and the fact that he always has Greek yogurt dripping out of his mouth.

A chapter about Stamos would be filled with stories of many women, many degrees of mullet, many more women, all the way through to his shorter hair with bangs—then more stories of women and bangs and then bangs and women. But that chapter is not going to be in this book.

This one will. True story: John and I once went into a bathroom at the Laugh Factory in Hollywood and stood next to each other at the urinals. There was another dude in there, a young guy who looked probably around eighteen.

So, out of nowhere/on purpose, John and I started to talk in character as Jesse Katsopolis and Danny Tanner. "Hey, Jesse, how's it going?" "Good, Danny. Having trouble getting Nicky and Alex to go to bed, but what you gonna do?"

The eighteen-year-old kid couldn't believe it. He peed all over himself. For just that instant, the poor kid thought *Full House* was real.

Another memorable time with John was spent in Las Vegas. Just the two of us. Schwing. He took me to see an Elvis impersonator at the Hilton, in the same showroom Elvis performed in. In tribute I got a little Elvis-style inebriated.

We were going to go to "the clubs" but I was done for the night. Instead, John had to take me back to one of three suites he had booked for the night—he always had backup suites in Vegas. Anyway, that night, he ended up literally taking off my shoes, cutting up my room-service steak, and feeding me so I wouldn't yack. One of his sisters even stopped by to check on us. Then he put me to bed. He went to bed soon after. Next to me.

When I woke up the following day I realized . . . I had just slept with John Stamos. And it was not the first time. I remember the first heartrending thing he said to me when we woke the next day: "My breath tastes like a piece of shit crawled into my mouth and took a shit."

Definitely not the Rat Pack. Maybe more like the Crap Pack. Boys will be boys.

I once wrote this down as a possible joke: "You know what separates the men from the boys? The police."

Before I end this chapter, I want to tell one last story, about probably one of the stupidest things I've *ever* done. How can that be after what you've just read? Seriously, I went into Inspector Clouseau territory with this one. It happened about ten years ago. My daughters were fifteen, twelve, and nine at the time.

It was right after knee surgery. I had torn my meniscus running on the beach. Only four miles, but I had come down on my knee stupidly like a semi-awkward man over forty can do. For all those screwed-up-knee guys who can relate, I ended up having arthroscopic surgery and wearing a cast.

Soon after the surgery, my dearest family friends invited me and my three daughters on a camping trip. It was a beautiful trip. We had guides with us—and two boats with a crew of four to go downriver . . . wait, that legally couldn't be called a "camping trip." It was what it was.

I was trying to enjoy myself but I just wasn't feeling well—still in pain, taking ibuprofen, as we do for these things. Finally, after a long day of journeying down the Colorado to the Snake River, four parents, seven kids, and four guides, we pitched our tents on a beautiful riverbed.

A crazy-indulgent, barely-roughing-it, fun trip. We stayed up late playing guitar and singing every Beatles song we could remember. The adults were drinking whiskey. Chivas Regal. I was hurting as it'd been a long day.

It got late. We had our sleeping bags set up under the stars on a little hill. I was trying the best I could to get to mine and everyone was helping me get there. There were two tented portable toilets set up about two hundred feet away. "One for pee" and "one for poo." It was easy to tell them apart. One smelled like shit.

As soon as the sun set, I'd kept warning all the kids: "Be very very careful if you have to go to the bathroom tonight. There could be snakes and you could hurt your feet in the dark." We all had flashlights, prepared for anything that could happen.

I was a mess and couldn't get to sleep. One of my friends had a sleeping pill and asked if I would like one. I'd never had one before. Truth. So I took my first Ambien. There's a reason for all the disclaimers in the ad. Do not drink and take a sleeping pill.

I went right to bed—with an ice pack on my aching knee—and whiskey in me as well as the first Ambien I'd ever taken. I do not remember much else of what happened except it ended horrendously. Two hours later, I woke up a zombie. I immediately had to piss. I have little memory of this but I know I got my flashlight and slowly, carefully as I could, started to limp alone to the bathroom on the sandy hill in the distance.

It was far. Felt like a mile. Probably two hundred yards. I got to the tented "for pee" toilet, which had a metal A-frame around it. As soon as I walked in to pee, I immediately did what I told my kids not to do—ridiculously jammed my foot into the A-frame and it split my toe wide open. On my bad leg.

I peed and then, with blood gushing out of my toe, drunk and on Ambien, ambled down the hill moaning loudly like a ghoul from hell. It woke everyone up. The kind guides rushed up and started right away to do first aid on my foot. Cleaning the wound, bandaging it until my toe looked like a turkey drumette. I was in some pain. It's cool we don't really remember pain.

Then they offered me a Vicodin. And I took it. Actually, I took two. Do not do any of this. You can die. At two A.M. I was a bloody hot mess. I slept for a few hours before the sun came up, as it tends to do. Everyone gathered around me, staring at the creature before them: A zombie. A zombie hungover on Ambien, Vicodin, and whiskey. I was the poster boy for "DON'T."

My dear friends and children helped me pack up my sleeping bag and dressed me in a long-sleeved shirt and a Gilligan hat— then they tried to put suntan lotion on me and placed me in the front of the boat we were traveling downriver in. I looked like the dead guy in my friend Jonathan Silverman's film *Weekend at Bernie's*.

I muttered some *Walking Dead*–type babble to my daughters and then slept like a mannequin from an out-of-business camping-supplies-store window, passed out for the two-hour river-rapids ride to our next destination.

By the time we got to the shore of the next campsite for the night, my mind started to come back. I sat in a lounge chair drinking filtered river water while my friends were fishing on the banks of the river. My dear friends' daughter went to cast her line into the water—but it suddenly hooked onto her mother's hat.

I saw this, got panicked like Lenny in *Of Mice and Men,* and on autopilot, leapt to my foot, yelling, *"I'LL SAVE YOU!!!"* Of course I had no balance—and fell back into the beach chair, somersaulting backward two times like a potato bug, landing flat on my back. Everyone laughed at me. The way you don't want to be laughed at. I finally knew what it felt like to be the first-prize winner on *America's Funniest Home Videos*.

I trust the things I've shared here have been received as more than just a whacked confessional and more entertaining than disconcerting. I'm obviously not bragging about this idiotic behavior. It bums me out when I meet young people who relish their stories of how fucked-up they get. And as I've previously mentioned, they want to get high or drunk with *me*. Honored some of you think I'm cool enough to warrant that, but my days of being a fucked-up zombie creature who somersaults backward on whiskey, sleeping pills, and Vicodin are over. I know, those are strong words. The words of a grown-up.

My mom told me fairly recently about a poignant dream she had. My father, who'd passed away several years before, came to her, she said, to tell her something he wanted us all to hear. The message he conveyed to her, that she wanted to impart to me, was:

"Stay alert. Pay attention." Okay, I'm doin' it, Dad.

Chapter 9

THE TEN-YEARS THEORY

My old joke used to be: "It's not good to name-drop; Robert De Niro told me that." I would occasionally mix it up and say, "Quentin Tarantino told me that." Actually, Quentin worked at a video store in the eighties that was right next to the Comedy and Magic Club, in Hermosa Beach, and several years ago reminded me I'd rented tapes from him back in the day.

I didn't remember any specifics so I asked him fearfully, "I didn't rent porn, did I?" He said, "No, man," and told me that when I'd come in we'd just talk about movies we loved. I was super relieved, and proud to hear my higher self was functioning that far back, since up until then I had self-diagnosed myself as being a perverted young bastard.

Here comes another name-drop. It was January 2003, and California governor Gray Davis was being sworn in. He was shortly after sworn out, but that's another story. I was asked to perform at a star-studded event for the big night in Sacramento— alongside musicians Lionel Richie, Kenny G, and Coolio. It was my first and only time doing stand-up at an inaugural event. This may sound a bit self-important, but I can't help but think perhaps my performance had something to do with the governor's impeachment.

Beloved actor and activist Edward James Olmos was also speaking that night. His speech was long and thoughtful—about the dangers of what was happening to our planet. Then he took my friend Michael and me aside and started to philosophize about the life of an artist and an actor.

His theory went something like this: "It takes ten years to get discovered, it takes another ten to do the work and have people embrace it, then it takes another ten years for you to fall out of favor with the people for a while. Then you have to reinvent yourself— and only then do they, the people, decide that it's their choice to discover you all over again. They want to think it was their idea, not yours. *They* rediscover *you.*"

Ten years, then ten years, then ten years. It was at that moment that I figured out Edward James Olmos was one hundred and twenty years old. He is the Immortal. I was recently reminded by my friend Michael that after Mr. Olmos finished describing his ten-years theory, he went on to talk to us about a variety of unrelated subjects, including 1) how easy it would be to poison our water supply, and 2) how on *Miami Vice* he'd been fortunate enough to hold full creative control over every scene he ever acted in.

I had been "Olmosed." And to this day, much of what he said makes sense to me. For one, I only drink bottled water.

Applying his ten-years theory to my own life, it kind of matches up. My career has certainly had a few different incarnations. It took me ten years to get a TV show on the air, and I wound up with two of them simultaneously. I was double-teamed by family TV.

In my own self-involved bubble, I felt like I'd waited longer than anybody I knew to get a job of consequence in show business. When you're struggling you think you're the only one. Later you realize how many people had it worse than you even at your lowest. Especially nowadays, it seems ludicrous.

I once had a comedian friend who had no dental coverage, and when he chipped his tooth and half of it broke off, he picked it up and glued it back on with Krazy Glue. It wasn't even like going to a dentist was an option.

There are some successful people who seem like they were always successful, like they've been unscathed by failure their whole lives—they rose to the top right away, didn't have to struggle to launch their careers. Like anyone on a hit reality show. But as my dad used to say, "That's just bullshit." And though we all trash reality shows, the good ones are, at their highest point, documentaries. I don't personally put anyone as talented as Anthony Bourdain or anyone on *Deadliest Catch* in the reality-show category. They are broadcasters and documentarians. To be clear, I wasn't just being facetious—if you can catch fish or cook fish, I'm in.

Even people who achieve sudden meteoric success probably went through times when they didn't think they'd make it. Even ten-year-old actors and eighteen-year-old singer-songwriters. All go through pain along the journey. It's true of any kind of artist or anyone seeking out a career in show business, as opposed to just fighting for instant celebrity. Most performers and entertainers will tell you they didn't arrive on schedule. Some are still waiting for their "arrival."

I have a memory of the moment when the dog that played Comet on *Full House* starred in the movie *Air Bud*. Stamos was like, "Fuck that dog! How'd the dog get a movie and not us?" A year later, the dog died. It's hard enough being an actor or actress and trying to keep your career alive another ten years . . . but if you only had a seventh of that time window? Without being aware of it, you live even more in the moment. Because you're a dog. He worked like a dog too.

A couple years ago, I saw a really funny comedian take the stage at the Improv, at a benefit my friend Kevin Nealon was hosting where every comedian performing that night had a disability. The first comedian up was in a wheelchair and could only move a couple fingers and his head. He wheeled up to the mic and his opening line was: "They told me if you masturbate you'll go blind. That's not what happened to me!"

You just can't get in and out of this life without something side-swiping you. You could be sitting by your beautiful pool thinking you're the shit and a bird could suddenly fly overhead and—SPLAT—you *are* the shit.

And if, through all fault of your own, you walk around, regardless, believing no matter what the circumstance that you *are* still the shit, stuff will inevitably happen in the universe to balance things out and set you straight. It's just how it goes.

To be clear, it's great to have confidence and love yourself. I'm only calling out the people who are flat-out arrogant, who think their farts smell like Chanel. I once knew a girl whose farts did smell like Chanel, but that's only because I inserted the bottle into her butt while she was asleep. Oh no, I "di-in't." Another phrase for you to remember: Do not insert things into anyone's butt while they're asleep.

If you're going through a time in your life when everything is burning on all four burners, firing on all eight cylinders, both of your balls working in synchronicity, yet independently of one another . . . savor it. The greatest moments in life are when your kids and the people you care about are doing well, your work is going well, your relationship is going well, and you have your health. If you're fortunate enough to have all those sectors of your life in a good place at once—friggin' high-five yourself and keep it rollin' as long as possible.

We mortals can lose our streak of confidence all of a sudden and fall off our game. No different than an athlete or model whose window of brilliance is shorter than that of people in other chosen professions. Yes, I just used the words *model* and *brilliance* in a sentence.

Someone not too long ago walked by me on the street and said, "Bob, you are the shit." And I answered sincerely, "Thank you for adding the *the*."

I've been on both sides of the equation. There have been times when people thought I was the shit. And there have been times when I thought someone else was the shit. When I was younger, I sometimes didn't know how to act around people whose work I worshipped. Here's a relatively brief example.

After my first appearance on *The Tonight Show Starring Johnny Carson*, I was asked back but got bumped from the show because they ran out of time. The guests that night were Jimmy Stewart, Roddy McDowall, and bluesman Preston Smith. I was a little nervous but what I remember through the nerves is arriving at the show, beyond excited, and then being told by the talent coordinator, Jim McCawley, that I had been bumped.

I was disappointed of course but got over that quickly when Jim asked me if I wanted to meet Jimmy Stewart. He took me into the makeup room and there was one of my movie idols sitting in the chair with Kleenex coming out of his shirt collar.

Jim was very kind and told Mr. Stewart that I was a nice young comedian who had gotten bumped that night. Jimmy Stewart shook my hand and said, "Well, niiice to meeeet ya . . ." I stammered back how amazing it was to meet him and then I did what some people do when they are in awe—I stood and stared at him, saying nothing, making him just uncomfortable enough. Probably a good seven interminable seconds went by with no dialogue.

The moment finally ended, to Mr. Stewart's benefit, and I walked away feeling like I'd just shaken the hand of God. I was getting ready to leave and go home when the producer of the show, the sweet Peter Lassally, came over to me and apologized for not getting me on the air that night. Peter was the main reason I got to be on *The Tonight Show* as a guest in the first place.

He felt so bad that, as he was escorting me out of the hallway, he asked if I would like to meet Jimmy Stewart, having no idea I had already just met the legend. I don't know why I did this—I guess I was that starstruck by the man who was George Bailey—but I acted as though I hadn't just met Mr. Stewart: "Yes, I'd love to."

Peter took me into the *Tonight Show* stage and there, behind a flat, was Jimmy Stewart again, now sitting in the dark backstage, a half hour before the show was to tape. Peter walked me over and introduced me for the second time in ten minutes (in James Stewart time), and explained to Mr. Stewart that I had been bumped that night.

Mr. Stewart said, "Welll, welll, wellll, didn't I jjjjust meeeet you before?" I couldn't lie to the man who starred in *Mr. Smith Goes to Washington*, so I said, "Yessir, I'm sorry, I just wanted to meet you again." I didn't stay too long this time or stare at him creepily. But I did notice him give me a justified look of concern afterward, as if saying, "Something's wrong with that boy." And he was right.

So yeah, I've done to people what gets done to me, but I ain't kidding myself, folks. I know I ain't no Jimmy Stewart. That would be Tom Hanks. I'm just saying I get that occasional fan who thinks of me that way.

I've been on both sides. I admit I acted like a sycophantic wanna-be hanger-on with Jimmy Stewart. And I admit it's satisfying sometimes to be around people who think you're cool, for whatever reason. But what I don't go for is fame-seeking and superficial relationships or materialism and self-indulgence, and the kind of people who flock to that lifestyle. I've been involved with too many people like that. One of my foibles I'd say I'm guilty of is being a talent whore. But deifying Jimmy Stewart falls under its own special air.

Some thoughtful people who've made a lot of money will tell you: money doesn't bring you happiness—but it does make your life easier. And some of the wealthy bitch-boys in the world will tout a variation: "money isn't everything—it's the hookers and blow you buy with money that are everything." These boys are just adorable. Makes me wish I had a son. To cut off.

Back to what sells books: I have never been with a hooker. I mean, I've been in the same room as a hooker, but I've never paid for sex. Well, I've had sex with someone and paid for everything they've asked me to pay for, but they weren't a hooker.

Okay, I just looked up the word *hooker* in the Urban Dictionary—

"prostitute, started in the Civil War when Gen. Hooker of the Union Army (the first pimp) tried to protect his troops from VD by buying the best chicks and pimping them to his corps of 20,000 men. Originally hooker's girls." Oh yeah, sorry, I wasn't totally correct. I did pay for sex once with a woman who'd been with twenty thousand men during the Civil War. She just laid there. A good mummy will do that.

A fortunate few on this earth have *never* had money concerns. Never even had to work. Trust-fund kids. And some of them are very nice people. Some of my relatives have wanted to know about anyone rich and famous I've met over the years. They ask, "Are they nice?"

"Well, Cousin Sheryl, I actually heard he is cruel to women and not much of a father." And her response would be, "Oh, okay. But is he *niiice*?"

I used to envy people born into money, because I was not. But at some point along the way I began to appreciate the value of being self-made, of starting from nothing and turning into something. And I know that's subjective. I couldn't be prouder that I was a deli clerk for five years while I finished high school and supported myself working through college.

I couldn't be prouder that I lived in a single apartment and had a strong inherited work ethic that propelled me to just keep moving forward even though the future occasionally looked bleak. And I couldn't be prouder of how many people I've been able to support because I was fortunate enough to have some luck grace my career.

What the fuck am I talking about? Trust-fund kids rock!! I wanna be the Facebook twins!! Who doesn't? Yikes. Truth is, if I'd have been a trust-fund kid I wouldn't have had the experience of getting to know my noble father and all the hardships he boldly faced. Then again, I'd have been getting laid since I was thirteen and flown on jets to Paris instead of working in that fucking deli . . .

Nah, my dad was right. It's all bullshit. I would not trade a moment in this life that got me to where I am today—and to where I will be tomorrow.

Whatever your journey is, it's *your* journey. And most people have, through no fault of their own, very difficult journeys. And it's not because their series didn't get picked up. That kind of thinking makes you wanna throw up in your mouth again, doesn't it?

Actually, no, that's a bad expression. Nothing makes me wanna throw up in my mouth. All right, one thing does: young girls who say, "That makes me wanna throw up in my mouth."

The best things in life often happen when you're not trying so hard. There were times I was busting my ass so hard to break through the door and nothing would budge. Then there were times when the door just opened and the opportunities arrived.

Other times, things came in through the door but it was basically the "doggy door"—something entered my life uninvited, like a crazed squirrel getting in through those dog flaps. Nothing worse than a crazed squirrel who breaks into your house through the doggy door, shits right in your living room, and eats your puppy. And then leaves the same way he came in . . . through the dog flaps. Never will see that again in print . . . dog flaps.

Even if it doesn't feel like it at the time, the hard work eventually pays off. But we never appreciate things while we're going through them. Time is the bastard. You take it on faith, you take it to the heart, the waiting is the hardest part.

Weird that most people in show business complain if they're

working . . . or if they're not working. Better to be able to complain about the former. Smarter not to complain at all. And yet I was prone to complain . . . for so many years of my career I felt like my comedic nut was not being cupped.

One of my nuts was happy-go-lucky and appreciative, but the other was confused and angry over unrequited moments in comedy it felt it was missing. And there's one thing you want out of life as a male artist: for both nuts to find a happy medium.

Rodney Dangerfield was a guy I would go to for Yoda-like advice. He'd been beaten down so much; he knew what it meant to be a survivor. Talk about the ten-years theory—he went from being named Jacob Cohen to changing it to Jack Roy to finally being dubbed Rodney Dangerfield. Years and years of television appearances, club after club, before catching his biggest break in *Caddyshack* at the age of fifty-nine, which led to a monumental resurgence with his doing exactly the kind of comedy films he wanted to do.

One time when he was living at the Beverly Hilton, I went over to his place, walked in, and started venting about how I was frustrated creatively—even with my two hit shows on the air, both being in the top ten.

I told him I was sick of only doing "family stuff" and wanted to move into edgier comedy but that I was concerned it was too late, because people have a way of branding you with what they perceive you to be. I went off to him about how the commercial shows had gotten so big that I thought it would be impossible for people to ever see me in a different comedic light.

Rodney listened to me intently, then looked at me with his big intense eyes and told me, with these exact words: "You don't know *cock*." I just stared at him. I'd never heard the word *cock* used to replace the word *anything* before. And with that unique turn of phrase, he set me straight.

He told me how he'd struggled and how long it took for him to get through his various stages. And how long it continued to take him to get to his next stages. I valued his frankness. His wisdom was only slightly diminished by the fact that he wore a robe all day long, and as he'd adjust his robe, his balls would occasionally peer out to see how things were going. Though it was distracting, his wisdom was my takeaway.

There's one funny story about Rodney that people always ask me about, wanting to know if it's true—and it is. This happened like twelve years ago. I'd called Rodney and scheduled a dinner with him for the following Wednesday at seven. I was going to take him to the Palm for a lobster. He was pissed at the Palm because ten years earlier he'd ordered a lobster and they brought him one with one giant claw and one little claw.

He was still angry about it and hadn't been back since. "Imagine, man, they did it on purpose! One big claw and one little claw!!" I tried to explain that I didn't think it had been on purpose; shit like that just happens.

Eventually, I got him to agree to give them a second chance. We made a plan. I was to take him to the Palm and get him a lobster with two giant claws. All was cool till I showed up a week later at his condo on Wilshire Boulevard at exactly 7:01 P.M.

There was an elevator that took you right up to his apartment. I rang the bell and was greeted at the door by Rodney, in a robe—open as always, and you could see his junk hanging out. Not a pretty picture, especially before dinner. But Rodney was Rodney.

His wife was on her way out with a friend. Rodney was shocked to see me. "Bob, what are you doing here?" I reminded him we'd made dinner plans.

"But you didn't call to confirm, man." He felt terrible because he had assumed our plans were off—since I hadn't called to confirm—and instead invited the porn star Ron Jeremy up to his place. It was for Ron to sign a one-sentence release so Rodney could use him in his book.

Ron was a huge fan of comedy who also happened to be famous for being a man with the ability to go down on himself. Not a tall man, but apparently a limber man—like a roly-poly pill bug. With no spine. And a gigantic penis. Don't see how I'd have any trouble getting him to sign a release for this book after that description.

Rodney invited me to stay and hang out with Ron and the two women he was bringing—"Sorry, man, I didn't think you were coming, so I invited Ron Jeremy and two hookers up for a little while to hang out." He offered me a joint.

"Sorry, Rodney, I think I'm just gonna go home. I don't do well hanging out with hookers, and Ron Jeremy always wants to shake my hand when I run into him at the Comedy Store and I always picture where it was right before the handshake."

I told Rodney I had nothing against Ron and explained I'm just a bit OCD. Told him, "It's cool, man, I gotta go."

As Rodney walked me to the elevator he adjusted his robe and I saw the huge long scar down the middle of his chest where, just a couple years earlier, they had apparently—as he described it—taken all of his guts out, laid them next to him, and then put them back in.

There he was, standing in front of me, sad that I was leaving, and waiting for Ron Jeremy and two ladies of the evening. As I got in the elevator I looked at him with all sincerity and asked him, "Rodney, how are you doing?"

He gave me a Rodney look. "You wanna know how I'm doing, Bob? I'll tell you how I'm doing. *You're* leaving, and I'm waiting for a guy who can suck his own *COCK*, that's how I'm doing!"

And then, as if timed for the perfect take, the elevator doors slowly closed as we both realized how funny what he'd just said was.

It's all about surviving. And getting back up after you get knocked down. The band Chumbawamba said it best: "I get knocked down, but I get up again. You're never gonna keep me down. I get knocked down, but I get up again. You're never gonna keep me down." How can you refute something so positive and motivational, recited in that song a thousand times and performed so eloquently by Chumbawamba?

"My Way" and "That's Life" have always been my musical mantra go-tos. Sinatra had the ultimate swagger: "I've been up and down and over and out, but I know one thing—each time I find myself flat on my face, I pick myself up and get back in the race . . ."

That's a lovely metaphoric lyric. Taking it literally would be taking it to extremes, but it's fun to riff about. Imagine you're running in a marathon and you trip over your feet and fall flat on your face. Then imagine every other runner racing past you, and your nose is broken beyond recognition, blood gushing out of it.

All you can see, out of your blurry peripheral vision, are these people running past you. Some even step on you and crush your ribs because they don't see you on the ground lying flat on your face. So you summon all your emotional strength and confidence to pick yourself up and . . . get back in the race.

Now imagine you're running alongside the other runners again. But now it's the very end of the race, and the runners speeding past you to the finish line are only the incredibly slow or way overweight ones. Doesn't matter, you're right there with them. You did it. You may have come in last, but you're not alone. There are other losers there with you. And you just "picking yourself up and getting back in the race" makes you a winner.

And through that blood gushing out of your nose, and your broken and battered body, you start to sing to yourself, kind of like Sylvester the Cat after he gets smashed to smithereens: "Thhhatttssthh liifffeee . . . Thtataathhhs whaatt all the pppaah-pppaah-peeeoplle tthhhhaayyyy."

The spirit of that song tells you, you know you're gonna get over it. Even though you pretty much feel like shit for about a year because you chose to follow the lyrics literally and you picked yourself up and got back in the race and were trampled over.

And then you wonder—maybe you shouldn't have gotten back in that race. Maybe if you were going through such a tough time in your life, you should've skipped the marathon that year and just gone right to the neighborhood bar and drunk your pain away. Watched the race on TV.

But you didn't. And you learned. And now you know. There's always next year. And if you're not so imbecilic as to fall flat on your face at the start of the race next time, you could even finish with the runners who come in first, near the *front* of the race. That's what drives people to move forward, the belief that with hard work, you too can be number one.

And if not, then at least you learn from it being ingrained in you that day—that, okay, you are a loser—and it's okay not to be number one. Then you can finally embrace *that*. Maybe even stop needing to be in races. Maybe racing's not your thing. Maybe it's badminton or chess, or being a chicken mascot at a Little League game . . .

And maybe, just maybe, you don't have to base your life on lyrics from a Frank Sinatra song. Just 'cause Frank was the Chairman of the Board is no reason to have to follow his every lyrical command. Or if you still have to worship Frank and all his lyrics, perhaps try other Sinatra songs: "All of Me," "The Lady Is a Tramp," and eventually, you can get to "It Was a Very Good Year."

These days I can't help but talk in this weird self-help, parental-type way. It comes from a real place. It's my genetic makeup. My daughters aren't just "beards" for me to look like a nice guy.

So with that in mind, for all my young readers, I'll continue my Tony Robbins Jr. motivational rant for just a little longer if I may . . . This is assuming you're not older than me and looking for parental advice from this book. If you *are* older than me and looking for me to be your father figure . . . I'm flattered . . . and completely creeped out. But I am here for you, old sweet child of mine.

My biggest advice is, whatever you choose to do with your life, do something you love, whether you're going to be number one at it or not. Not everyone has to be number one. Coming in third on *The Biggest Loser* could be the biggest win of your life. Not to mention, it means you can go right back, the day after shooting, to your solid diet of thick-cut bacon and ice cream shakes. By the way, why would they call a show *The Biggest Loser*? Seems slightly mean, doesn't it?

But really, not everyone can be number one. Look at me, I'm not great at sports. I like 'em. I *love* going to a game, but playing most group sports was never my thing. It's kinda fucked-up to have to admit that in a book. There are so many good athletes out there. I have jock envy. I was always itching to be a jock.

That's not to say I haven't had some decent luck in public a few times. I can par a hole-in-one every ten years and then lie fifteen every hole after. Gimme a golf cart and a cigar and I'm a happy man. And an honest man. I never lie about a hole.

Teed up by my dear athletic actor/director friend Jonathan Silverman, I once got an RBI at a Hollywood All-Stars celebrity charity baseball game. I was at Dodgers Stadium, I hit the ball, and I ended up with turf toe. That means I ran so hard my toenail came off in my shoe. Spaz attack. But I made it to first base.

John Salley was there to meet me as the first baseman. I jumped up, clinging to John, and his comment, coolly, to me was, "Are you the new Jewish kid in the neighborhood?" Sandy Koufax I was not.

So there you have it, no hiding anymore. I'm out now as a guy who under the heading of "sports" on his acting résumé listed all the things he was actually pretty good at: biking, swimming . . . biking . . . walking, sitting, lying, oh, and standing.

When I was eight I was playing football with a bunch of kids. The ball got thrown to me and I panicked and ran the other direction. Got a touchdown for the opposing team. They have names for kids who do that. Mine was "Fag."

And the first syllable of my last name was an assist. But I got knocked down and I got up again. Because you're never gonna keep me down. Thank you, Dad. Thank you, Rodney. And thank you, Chumbawamba.

We get up and reinvent ourselves. We all have stuff happen that detours us from what we expect. But every morning there's—in addition to morning wood—the faith that the new day will let positivity and growth into our lives. It's always safer to not take chances and to not get your heart broken and try your best to not break someone else's. I've never taken the safe route.

GPS is a good metaphor for "safe-routing." I've driven with my car's GPS and my iPhone's GPS on simultaneously, and both of their lady voices go out of their way to fuck me up. Especially when I'm driving across ancient American Indian grounds. That's a true fact that I think we can both be thankful I am not expounding upon.

I used to always make it more difficult for myself to get to where I wanted to go. Not anymore. I cut to the chase quicker. Doesn't always go as I'd like it to go, but I try to waste less time. Time is the most valuable commodity. More valuable than tires.

The Greek playwright Aeschylus was correct when he wrote, "Wisdom comes alone through suffering." I don't know if his plays were ever successful. But he wrote some good shit.

As I've mentioned, I've always felt throughout my life that I was ten years behind. Okay, not at ten. That's why I enjoyed being ten. Didn't feel like I was still held back at zero years old.

Admitting in this book that I've always felt ten years behind is tough for me. Concerned it's too personal. And throughout the process of writing this, I've often experienced these moments of hesitation—not just because the material is personal but because I imagine other people who may be reading this who've been through their own hard times.

That's why I haven't wanted to write a book until now. I'm honored you want to read my stories, even though I'm still deciding if I should write this book. It's probably a little late not to write it now, as this has already been published. We're past "just the tip" at this point. Do you feel anything? Is it good for you? Am I in yet? Please don't look me in the eye and say my name.

Maybe in addition to the audiobook, I should release this in dry-erase board form. Or Colorforms. Just to give you the option to remove things as you see fit.

Getting back to the ten-year theory, none of us know in life what the next ten years are going to bring—in the world, in our health, work, family, relationships . . . Again, if you've got it all going on at the moment—your work is good, your family isn't a pain in the ass—then bless you. Freeze it, 'cause life is sweet. And it goes fast.

I've learned to appreciate those frozen moments. Life is like my sperm. I want to freeze it sometimes. It's nice for the company. I'm cherishing my life right now, because as soon as I get into the next lascivious chapter, as life imitates art, some weird shit will end up in my life just as I'm writing about weird shit.

Every few years, work shows up in my life completely unannounced. A couple of those types of career moments changed me as a person just as much as if I'd been in a long-term relationship.

When I lost my sister Gay to scleroderma in 1994, I wanted to share our family's story with others and let them know they weren't alone in this battle. So in 1996 I directed a television movie for ABC called *For Hope*, starring Dana Delany, that was "loosely based" on events that "directly" affected my family. It was a very emotional and fulfilling project and a poignant moment in my life, one I will always treasure.

That TV movie helped put scleroderma on the map and inspired me to continue working toward the effort to fund research for the disease. At the time, Oprah graciously devoted a half-hour of her show to the telefilm: She had me on, along with Sharon Monsky, the founder of the Scleroderma Research Foundation. Sharon had played herself in the film, and Dana Delany was brilliant as Hope, a woman stricken in her prime with this prevalent but still largely unknown disease.

The great experience with *For Hope* made me want to direct more. I did a few TV movies—*Jitters, Becoming Dick*—and I loved making them . . . but the wildest experience, without question, was the Norm MacDonald comedy feature I made for MGM, called *Dirty Work*.

Norm claims I was the first comedian he ever saw when he was a teenager in Ottawa. Yes, I met Norm MacDonald when I was twenty-one and he was only seventeen. I remember picking on this smart-looking kid near the front row of a club and razzing him over his large hair-fro. Years later, I got to know Norm better. I had hosted *Saturday Night Live* and when he needed a director for the script he'd cowritten, he decided I might be the right guy. *Dirty Work* is about two guys, played by Norm and Artie Lange, who open a revenge business to try to raise fifty grand to buy a new heart for their dad, played by the amazing Jack Warden.

We shot the movie in Toronto, and part of the modus operandi was that everybody had to behave. Artie Lange had to stay clean and sober, and we had to bring in all the renegade comedy actors as quickly and efficiently as we could so they could get in and out before their loved ones and the government knew they were gone.

I was dealing with my own personal stuff at the time, going through a divorce—flying my daughters and parents to Toronto so I could spend some time with them.

The movie had a cool cast that's an honor to name-drop: Chris McDonald, the great late Chris Farley, Traylor Howard, and Chevy Chase, with cameos by David Koechner, Adam Sandler, John Goodman, and an icon whom I have the pleasure of having become very close to since that movie was made . . . Don Rickles.

Don played the abusive movie theater owner. Norm and Artie and the other ushers in the theater were being verbally abused by Don's character, so their task was to screw him over—by switching the film *Men in Black* with *Men in Black: Who Like to Have Sex with Each Other.* The end result being the firing of the theater owner.

We were all in worship mode in the presence of Don, having been raised on his killer appearances on *The Tonight Show* and all of the Dean Martin roasts, in addition to having seen him perform live for years.

I caught some crap that day after aiming two cameras at Don and just letting him riff. With our two thirty-five-millimeter cameras, I used up several magazines of film on Don and was informed I'd gone through our whole film stock budget for the day. If only digital had existed, I wouldn't have been "disciplined."

The result was a classic scene edited by George Folsey Jr. of Don just ripping Artie apart: "So there you are, Tubby . . . You look like a bucket o' lard on a bad day . . . You baby gorilla . . . Why don't you work in a zoo and stop bothering people . . . I got a call yesterday from Baskin Robbins . . . They said that they're down to only five flavors . . . You're swelling up as I talk to you . . ."

It was hilarious. To this day, Don tells me he's always hearing from people how much they loved *Dirty Work* and how funny he was in it. He's told me more than a couple times that I'm one of the few directors who just let him go and do what he does. He says if only he'd known sooner how much people loved him in the film he would've tried harder to work with me in the ten years that followed.

Since then, through John Stamos—who's been very close with Don for a long time—I've gotten to know Don very well. I love him like a father. At this moment in time, he is the godfather of most of us stand-ups. It's not "old-school," it's just "school." Last year I had the great pleasure of honoring Don at the Friars Club dinner in New York. He is one of the last, if not the only, cuttingly on-mark, professional, kind, and dignified men who have ever done comedy.

A few years after we'd shot *Dirty Work*, I ran into Don at a restaurant in Santa Monica. He grabbed me and hugged me, held me as close as he could, and whispered in my ear so only I could hear . . . "I don't miss you at all."

Such a funny man. If you have a chance to see him live, do it now. Put down this book, go online, and buy tickets to wherever he is. He is one of a kind. A major influence in my life.

After directing a few more TV movies and some television

shows—one of my favorite being my friend Mike Binder's HBO series, *The Mind of the Married Man*—I got a call from Broadway. And it wasn't from a hooker on Thirty-Fourth Street. It was from her pimp.

In 2005, I was offered a role in this off-Broadway play at the Second Stage Theatre called *Privilege,* written by Paul Weitz. I loved every moment of it. It was a serious show about a man who goes to jail for insider trading. A seriously well-written play.

One of the performances wasn't as serious. It had been closed-captioned for the hearing impaired. I hadn't followed the script exactly, and the audience started to laugh, but only when my character spoke. It helps to be off-book. The hearing-impaired were much less impaired than I was at doing my lines while they were reading them. The play had been copied into the closed-caption monitors previously. Whatever, at that performance, my lines did not match what the audience was reading.

Working on *Privilege* changed me as an actor and as a person. I got some stripes in acting. Loved the people I got to work with. And I also learned it's probably not best to participate in insider trading.

But the next experience I had with Broadway was even more thrilling. My old executive producer from *Full House,* Bob Boyett, reached out to me to take over the lead role of an amazing show, *The Drowsy Chaperone,* playing the character called "Man in Chair."

My mother's response was, "You couldn't get a bigger part? I mean, he doesn't even have a name. He's just a *man in a chair*?" I banned her from the theater. Actually, she couldn't make the trip to New York because we'd just lost my dad and she was afraid to travel all that way and sleep in a strange bed alone. I told her I'd arrange for an old stage-trained actor to sleep with her every night and pretend to be my father, but she still wasn't enticed.

The incredible Bob Martin wrote this play and had eloquently originated the role of "Man in Chair." I was the last of several Man in Chairs. Before I'd even arrived to replace the Man In Chair, the show had already garnered five Tony Awards during its two-year run.

I made many friends during this experience. Such good friends that one day I showed up to work with the flu to give it to them all. I'd taken NyQuil the night before and was still pretty heavily on it by morning. When you're staggering to the bathroom in the middle of the night to take a swig of NyQuil and you have work in the morning, I'd recommend turning on the light to see how much you consume.

Sorry, I'm going back on my drug soapbox—do not show up to your Broadway play on NyQuil. You may not be congested but you won't know where the fuck you are.

Out of roughly eighty performances, this was my least professional moment during this life-changing Broadway experience. This is what happened on that NyQuil morning . . .

I showed up to rehearsal an hour early and immediately got into my wardrobe—a cardigan sweater and cords. Even pre-mic'd my glasses so I was able to hide the microphones in my large eyewear. I sat there for an hour waiting for the stagehands and cast to assemble. An actor in work mode can be like a Pavlovian trained animal. I was a seal on cold medicine.

The play had no intermission, and I was doing okay, remembering all my lines and hitting my cues, though I later found out I was talking at a slower pace than I had ever spoken at in a performance of the show. By the way, on Broadway, there is no just "okay."

Then the problem came. It was a fantasy play, all within the Man in Chair's head. At the end of the show there was a scene where the entire cast of twelve people were frozen waiting for my line. I was fed my cue: "What is that?" My answer was supposed to be . . . "A record." Seems simple enough. The cast waited, the brilliant well-established Broadway actors—a couple of them in the "more mature" age bracket. I couldn't keep them waiting. But I did. Not by choice.

I couldn't come up with the answer to "What was that?" I stared at them all. Almost as though I was gazing at Jimmy Stewart decades earlier—it was an eternity. My friend, the perfect actor Danny Burstein, started to glare, his eyes trying to squeeze the line out of my lips through his frozen statuesque pose. And then, I finally said it: " . . . A record . . . ?"

I think the entire audience could feel the exhaling of the cast wafting over them.

The reason I relay this story is it explains why I loved being on Broadway so much and why I definitely want to return. Not one person in the cast or company mentioned the NyQuil incident to me for weeks. Then one day, we were hanging around and one of the actors made a joke, to which the punch line was, "At least Bob wasn't on NyQuil."

It was then I pumped them for information on the show that I had no memory of. The moral here is similar to every other moral in this book. This one specifically is: Don't take NyQuil while on Broadway.

So a lot can happen in ten years. People's perceptions of you are their perceptions, but they don't define who you are and who you have to be. Unless you're into that sort of thing. If you are, wanna go camping?

If you've been around awhile in the entertainment field, people say stuff to you with no ill intent that you're not prepared for. Over the years I've had people come up to me and ask, "What are you doing now?" One time I answered, "Right now? I'm talking to you." They didn't know what to do with that information. My intention was to be in the moment and not be pricky about it.

I mean, it was an honest question. At the time I thought my answer was better than saying, "Oh, I've been making porn films with your sister." I don't think that would've sat well with that lady who drove all the way from Long Island to see the guy from *Full House* be in a Broadway show that she had heard good things about from her friends.

Sometimes when people ask me what I'm working on now, I get the "good luck with that" comment in return. Granted, I'm an overly sensitive guy, but just once in a while it's hard to tell if "good luck with that" is meant sincerely and sweetly or if it's meant how it sounds—as if the person is actually saying what their face looks like it's saying . . . "I just ate bad fish."

Anything good is hard. But enough about my penis. Show business definitely has its ten-year ups and downs. That is, if you're lucky enough to get ten years out of it in the first place.

It's pretty easy to tell how someone is doing in show business. If they're doing well, you will see them on the side of a bus. If they're *not* doing well, you will see them *inside* of a bus. Here's to another ten more years.

Chapter 10

THE ARISTOCRATS, ENTOURAGE, AND GETTING ROASTED

A'ight, I'm writing this chapter from my pool while smoking a cigar. Sounds badass, but I'm in a thong and a tube top. Not true. V-neck and bathing suit. What are *you* wearing?

Sometimes I've ended up in a club that in the past wouldn't have accepted me as a member. Oh, to be popular. Over the course of my life I've spent a lot more time being unpopular. And why do we care about being popular? Those of you who don't care at all, let's start a club. I was the Phantom of three different high schools. Comedians are outsiders, and if you move town to town like I did during high school you became an outsider's outsider.

Living in Los Angeles or New York and being part of a "clique" is what some people strive to accomplish in their lives. Of course, it has nothing to do with anything, but I have no right to judge it, because for me it was fun once in a while. It's always been a love/hate affair with wanting to be accepted—being unpopular for a long time makes you secretly want to be able to *choose* whether or not to be part of the "coolest people alive" club.

And if you roll with those people in France or Italy, then your life has even more meaning. At least on Instagram it does. And yeah, it's fun for the privileged few to be on a yacht in the Caribbean over Christmas—as long as the yacht doesn't turn into the Carnival cruise ship that had poop backing up in it. They had to rewrite the Wikipedia definition of *poop deck* after that incident.

After being exposed on TV as a good guy I sometimes get offers to do something 180 degrees from the persona I projected on the family shows that hit. One of my first "opposite day" cameos was in the movie *Half Baked,* written by Dave Chappelle and Neal Brennan.

I was directing *Dirty Work* in Toronto and I'd read *Half Baked.* I wanted to direct *Half Baked* because I liked the script so much. I'm not a stoner but I've always appreciated stoner books and movies. *Half Baked* and *Dirty Work* had the same producer, Bob Simonds. So while I was directing *Dirty Work* I was asked if I would do this cameo in *Half Baked.* I immediately said yes without thinking about it. It required no thought because the couple lines I said stood out like a sore cock.

I was in *Half Baked* for barely thirty seconds, in a drug rehab scene where Dave Chappelle said, "I am here today because I'm addicted . . . to marijuana." Another rehabber, played by Dave Edwards, stood up and yelled, *"Marijuana!?* Man, this is some *bullshit!"* Then I stood up right after and proclaimed, "Marijuana is not a drug . . . I used to suck dick for coke!!"

That wasn't even the incriminating part in the scene. Immediately after I shouted that out, the rehabber yelled out even louder off camera, "I SEEN HIM!"

I continued: "Now, that's an addiction, man. You ever sucked some dick for marijuana?" Dave Chappelle thought about it and finally said, "No, I can't say I have." I finished my "scene" with "I didn't think so," and sat down.

The rehabber yelling out, "I seen him!" was not good for my character. That meant that he actually saw me sucking dick for coke.

Anyway, that line has followed me around ever since. I get shout-outs at airports, at a store with my daughters . . . The coda on this one is, if you're going to do a cameo in a movie, and that's your line—think about it first. It's one thing to have people yell out, "Danny Tanner!"—but it's a whole different thing if your claim to fame is that you sucked dick for coke.

Times have changed though. In the past ten years you can really, for real, suck dick for coke and then get a reality show that'll make you rich beyond your dreams. Oh, man, I'm feeling another retraction coming on . . . I'm going to go out on a limb now, because I think most people who suck dick for coke . . . are not rich. They just suck dick. For coke. Again, I am a very fortunate man. Did not have to do that.

I don't regret the *Half Baked* cameo in any way. It's kind of a shock-value badge of honor—the only gig that fell in my lap, so to speak, where I was cognizant of it being for shock value. But the fact that things I spend many years working on can have the same impact as something that took less than two hours to shoot does cause me to reel a bit.

So here's another moment that took only thirty minutes to film but became comedically poignant in my life. I've spent many hours discussing it in interviews and I want to discuss it in this book.

I've already shared the traumatic events surrounding the birth of my first child and the uncomfortable comedic comment I made to my friend Paul Provenza back in 1987 when he was visiting my family after the trauma was passing. It was because of our history together that years later, Paul says he thought of me early on to be part of a documentary he was directing, *The Aristocrats,* produced by Penn Jillette. He felt my comedic attitude toward "acts unthinkable" was in the proper bent mode that the movie was actually about.

The interesting thing about the whole *Aristocrats* experience for me was I didn't know what the movie really was, and I'd only heard the joke once, from comedian Dom Irrera. Dom and I were standing in front of the Improv in L.A. after doing sets and Dom said something to me like, "It's like the Aristocrats joke." I told him I'd never heard the joke before.

Dom said, "Are you serious? This joke was *made* for you. You're gonna *love* this . . ." He then went on to tell me the story of a family who is so desperate to make it in show business that they would skate in their own feces . . . Is this a good time for a bookmark?

People ask me to tell this joke all the time, and I've only been able to even start it a few times since I first told it for the documentary shoot in 2004. Dom was truly delighted to introduce me to the joke for the first time. And it did affect me. Because it's about an act—an "act"—that is so heinous, so horrific, that it touched that part of me that responds to taboo humor. It's the unimaginable. And it's not for everyone. It's like making a joke about any horrific incident where it's always too soon to tell it. And it was dementedly funny to me. And my telling it in that film was the second time I'd ever told it in my life. It's exhausting and needn't ever be told again.

A few times when I've done a charity event or a religious-themed benefit I've accidentally/on purpose just thrown in the setup for the small percentage of the audience in the room who loved the movie.

"A family walks into an agent's office . . . ," is the gauge to see how many people even *know* the joke. Just to "take their temperature," as it were. And more people know it than you'd expect. And it's not meant to be told anymore.

Nor do I want to tell it. But the theme of it, especially in this sometimes twisted world we live in, is relevant. And unfortunately, it gets more relevant with every second of news footage we watch—and every police drama that exists, and fortunately only subliminally in a few reality shows. That's the one area they don't hit on too often on those shows—incest doesn't play well with people who participate in it. I just ran my fingers through my hair in a Bill Maher–like fashion.

The point of the film was not to display vulgarity. It was to hold up a mirror to a culture that believes in freedom of speech and yet . . . I've grown accustomed to her face. Wait, I don't want to get all political about this. Look, it's just something I was asked to do by two comedy artists I trusted, and so I participated, as though I was being asked to sit in with a jazz group one night. Except I don't play jazz. I appreciate it, but I only know four chords, and they're all G.

Telling the Aristocrats joke is like performing jazz. It's scat.

Interestingly or noninterestingly enough, the word *scat* has two meanings. And they both apply to this joke and the film. Jazz and poo. I'm coining it here: *jazzpoo*.

I hosted a show I liked on NBC once for a couple short seasons called *1 vs. 100*. On that show I coined the word *shiggles*. Yeah yeah, I've read your comments—I know it's obvious I was combining the words "shits and giggles" in prime time. The censors had no field day. That was my edgiest in a prime-time game show.

One of the best renditions of the Aristocrats story was told by my pal Gilbert Gottfried, and what's beautiful about it is it was done accidentally, because he wasn't doing very well on his unairable portion of the Friars Club roast of Hugh Hefner. Gilbert's a very sensitive person. Such a funny guy. He goes to a dark place immediately. There's a lot of complication with someone who starts there.

I love comedians whose comedy comes from pain. Most comedians have bouts with pain and so it's no surprise the people who excelled in the Aristocrats movie understood pain and comedy and how they intersect.

There were plenty of comedians in the movie who turned it down, who chose—intelligently—to *not* tell the joke. Including some of the best comedians who exist, like Chris Rock and Don Rickles. But I had no choice but to tell the joke. It was actually freeing for me. And I really didn't know what I was doing.

I'd been boxed into family comedy for so long, and just felt like I had fallen out of touch with whatever edgy comedic voice I had, that there was some weird morphing that occurred when the joke came out of me that day.

So Paul and Penn had set it up explaining they were interviewing a hundred comedians telling this same joke. I went to film it at the Laugh Factory one night and slated a set to do after the shoot. I needed to talk to them before we filmed to make sure I even remembered the details of the joke. Again, it was the second time I'd ever told it. With good reason.

In the film it looked like I was just spewing the obscene story, but what you didn't hear were Penn and Paul egging me on, yelling at me off camera: "Tell it!" "Go for it!" They cut out their off-camera comments. They had to egg me on because I really didn't want to tell it. That's kind of the joke. But once they got me wrangled, I delighted in their odd world of what was great about the film's concept.

In the joke (deep breath) the family goes into an agent's office— and to entice him to sign them as clients of his agency . . . they have sex with each other. They would possibly be the biggest winner ever on *America's Got Talent.* Maybe they'd have to create a new show so that families all over America could come in and compete. "Who will be the sexiest family in America? . . . Who will it be . . . the Andersons from Connecticut, or the Chesterfields from Kentucky?" By the way, those are random made-up names.

My go-to disclaimer in this book applies here as well: for a little while I was not sure whether to write about that joke or the movie because, more than anything I've ever done, it truly crossed all lines. But that was obviously the point of it. The telling of the joke was the task, and George Carlin made it clear this was not a funny joke, nor was it something that should be told anywhere but in some alley behind a Dumpster.

The punch line isn't a punch line. After the family finishes their "act," the agent says, "And what do you call yourselves . . . ?" I never delivered the punch line on-screen in the film. I had to leave just as I was about to say it, as I was cosmically announced to go onstage. I never got to tell the punch line in a documentary based on an "opposite day" punch line.

Months went by and my friend and then-manager Michael Price and I sat in the conference room at my management company to approve or disapprove the use of me in the film. I hadn't signed the release after I left the shoot. I'd wanted to see it first. I knew before and after I'd filmed it that this thing could be funny and not be a problem, or it could stain me and tarnish me. That's got to be the name of a porn film somewhere.

Since I wouldn't sign the release until I saw myself in the film, a screening was set up for Michael and I to watch it in a conference room with one of the producers. We were laughing all the way through my footage, which was intercut with Chris Albrecht, the then-head of HBO, as well as my comedienne friends Carrie Snow and Cathy Ladman—who all spoke affectionately about me and how I would go to a sicker place than anyone else would for the sake of sick humor.

I recall being surprised that my peers perceived me this way. It was weird hearing that I had this reputation. I didn't even feel that way about myself. I don't feel that way about myself now.

The film ended. I must confess during my part I'd had my hand over my eyes. I looked up and said to Michael, "Yes?" He said, "Yes. If you're okay with it, I'm okay with it." CUT TO: "And what do you call yourselves?"

I know I'm still dropping more names in this book than Cheez Doodles out of a goat's butt, but here's another one . . .

Doug Ellin, who wrote and created the show *Entourage,* called my managers soon after I'd shot my appearance in *The Aristocrats,* asking if I would play myself in an episode of the hit HBO show, which had been on for one year at that point. My friend Cliff Dorfman worked for Doug and stayed on him to make it happen that first time.

Doug had known me when he was just starting out and I was a stand-up who, as he relays it, was "balls-out." One of the things people loved about *Entourage* was how it pulled the veil off of people who were sometimes perceived as a Goody Two-shoes in the world. Their guest cast got to fuck with perceptions of themselves and it was fun.

Another persona do-over for me was about to happen. Doug's take was to portray me as myself, and he developed the character of "me" with me, who became, through his perspective, to be "the richest muthafucker with the biggest balls ever." I said, "Okay."

The first episode I was in, I showed up at Vincent Chase's house with a basket full of muffins and *Full House* DVDs. The thing that got ad-libbed on the set and that Doug wanted me to cultivate as a line was directed at Vincent, played by Adrian Grenier.

Guys who loved the show also say this to me way too often. They are no longer boys. They are men now. And, as I've said, they quote lines to me from various works I've done, but this one, out of context, can also be really awkward: "Yeah, come over anytime. But hey, don't fuck my daughters . . . Don't you fuck 'em . . ." Ironically, I've said that word ad nauseam in my stand-up, but not much as a verb.

Entourage depicted a much more despicable me than I am capable of being. It's not really a side of me at all, just a fictionalized version of me, that was a fun turn. In this case, life does not imitate art. The only thing I am guilty of is: I *have* stood in my backyard by the pool with a girlfriend nearby—and yes, I was unshaven, wearing a black robe and smoking a cigar. But character-wise I don't have the makeup to naturally treat a woman as an object. Maybe that's why it was so much fun to play—imitating myself imitating myself.

One time I was in the Rose Bar at the Gramercy Park Hotel in New York with two of my daughters and Jeremy Piven was also there with a nice young lady. Jeremy, of course, played Ari Gold on *Entourage*.

The point of the setup here is I had to leave for a moment to go to the bathroom, leaving Jeremy and his date with my daughters. And it just came out. I told him I'd be back and was leaving my daughters with him and then we all looked at each other and the same line came out of our mouths at the same time: "Don't you fuck my daughters." He pointed at me in the Ari kind of way.

My daughters are amazing, always ahead of the curve with their father, who has a teenage boy's demeanor. I went to the men's room and was back in less than two minutes. When you're out with your daughters in a bar, your bathroom breaks are uncomfortably short.

There is another story from when I was guesting on *Entourage* that I want to share but probably shouldn't. Man, I have used that device a lot in this book—if you really want to get someone's attention, tell them, "I really shouldn't be telling you this . . ."

Well, now that I've got your attention, let me tell you about this time I was preparing my scene with a lovely actress on the show. She was playing a woman who—in my heightened version of myself—in all likelihood was going to sleep with me. In preparation she wanted to discuss our characters before we went to set.

There wasn't much to discuss. I was a playing a misogynist

asshole version of myself—double take—and she was playing the part of a hot Ukrainian model. She asked me several questions so we could discuss our relationship: "Do we like each other?" "Yes." "Are you nice to me?" "Yes." And then came the only question that gave me pause . . . "Do you love me?" I felt bad for a second, because this heightened version of me went by my real name. And then I answered her . . . "No." And she was okay with that. My life has never been that simple. Like I said, I'm an overly sensitive guy.

Once again, they had written dialogue for me that I still get shout-outs over in public places. Some of my dialogue with E, played by Kevin Connolly, went exactly like this:

"Don't think I'm weird when I tell you this."

"Anything, Bob."

"Promise you won't call me weird?"

"Just say it, Bob. I won't call you weird."

"I want to have sex in Murray's office."

"What?"

"Yeah. I want to fuck her in Murray's office."

"Look, I get it, Bob. I'm sorry if we wasted—"

"I'm serious. I'm not weird, I'm pragmatic. This would be great for my memoirs . . ."

And that's the story of how I met your mother.

Is it humiliating to have people come up to me on the street to this day and say, "I want to fuck her in Murray's office?" Not usually, unless a guy named Murray is within earshot.

Several years back, I was subjected to possibly the most intense round of humiliation ever . . . I'm referring to the Comedy Central roast that bore my name and will live long in infamy. In-fo-me.

I used to love watching the Dean Martin roasts. When I was

young I would also listen to audiotapes of the Friars as well as other roasts—where I'd hear all the biggest comedy and movie stars in the world cursing in ways I'd never imagined. Fifteen-year-old boys love that humor. Hearing Jack Benny saying, "Tell him to go fuck himself," made me love him even more. Jack Benny was my father's favorite comedian. And obviously one of mine. Not for that one instance of hearing him curse. He was just a comedy genius who knew himself so well, the audience knew and adored him too.

I loved how loose the old roasts were. Something about the boys'-club aspect of it just allowing people to screw around with their friends. In retrospect, it's maybe one of the reasons I developed the style of comedy I've ended up with. Having a structure—but just riffing through it and bouncing off your buddies.

But as much of a fan as I am of the roasts, I am a man who never wanted to get roasted or do the roasting. I don't actually enjoy performing mean comedy. A writer friend of mine told me he thinks I use dirty jokes as a placeholder for what would otherwise be pit bull humor that I'm not comfortable doing. At the risk of sounding self-righteous yet again, I'm too positive and frankly too sensitive to be mean-spirited. Although one of my survival handicaps is, if someone throws one rock at me, I'll get catapults to throw a thousand back.

Basically, my philosophy is, like Rodney used to say, "Make fun of yourself first, then you can go after the audience." Over the years I did a couple private roasts for charity benefits, but I never *liked* making fun of people. Especially my friends. I wish some of my friends felt the same way. Okay, so the roast . . .

I'd seen all the previous Comedy Central roasts and didn't see this offer coming. I've been self-aware and honest about where I was and am in my career, so why did I need millions of people to see it reflected back to me? I'm not geared to sit in a room with a bunch of people and find out what's wrong with me and what mistakes I've made. If you crave that, all you have to do is go home for the holidays. Point is, I'm already my toughest judge.

That being said, I got the call from Comedy Central. To make my decision I watched every single roast they had done since they started doing them. Sometimes, it felt like the "It's over" club, and other times it was the "This is cool 'cause what the fuck do I care—there's an iconic thing to it" club. I chose the latter, but only if I could change up what they had done previously with most of those roasts. Make it more like the Dean Martin roasts, for *me* in my head at least—and have my actual friends on the dais.

A roast dais is supposed to have a podium in the middle of a Last Supper–like banquet table facing the audience. Except nowadays they set up these roasts to look like an airport lounge for Lufthansa, with an electric chair in the middle of it. That would be a good ending for the roast. Just electrocute the honoree. Oh, wait, they've done that.

My dear pal Jeff Ross wrote a book called *I Only Roast the Ones I Love,* taken from the famed Friars Club motto "We Only Roast the Ones We Love." That's a nice motto, and a good idea in theory, and sometimes in practice, but I will tell you, sometimes it burns.

Jeff's most quoted line about me in my roast was: "In honor of the late George Carlin, here are seven more words you can't say on TV: 'And the Emmy goes to Bob Saget.'" I heard that for the first time sitting in the roast chair. And I ain't gonna lie—it stung. And it was one of the best lines of the night.

That's what a Roast is. And Jeff's great at it. And I told him after: I'm gonna spend my life proving you wrong. It's a sweet and nasty little competitive group of alley cats I'm proud to be in. And I need it in my life to toughen my fruity little ass up.

So getting involved with the roasts not only made me learn how to take a hit, but it also made me so happy to follow in the footsteps—again, in my *own* mind—of my idols, like Dean Martin and Don Rickles.

And to have all my real comedy friends there, when I was being roasted, made it feel like family. The host was, of course, my brother John Stamos—I don't know if I've made it clear in this book yet that Stamos and I are close friends. Maybe I should just include a pic of us having sex. Oh, wait, I have one, here . . .

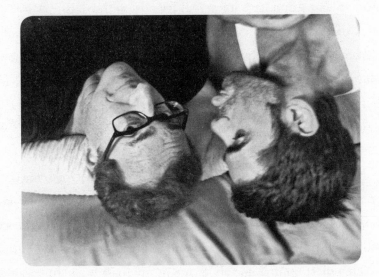

So John agreed to be the roast master, and he shared with me the kind of jokes the writers of the roast were suggesting for him to say about me, all with the underlying tone of "Bob Saget is a huge asshole!"

John stood up for me: "I told them I wanted to say nice things about you. I couldn't be mean to you like that, 'cause you're a great guy and I love you."

He had my back, and the intro was changed to: "Please welcome our guest of honor, the luckiest man and the worst entertainer in the history of show business. He's a huge asshole and one of my best friends . . . Bob Saget!"

Roasts are like punching someone and then putting ice packs on them. And I was just fine with that on this occasion.

Greg Giraldo. An incredibly funny man with a big heart. When I was told I was being roasted, the one person I feared was Greg. A lot of my friends had agreed to do it, and I knew what to expect from them.

But Greg . . . I'd met Greg, but we weren't "friends." "Acquaintances," a distinction my mom always made. His stand-up was really smart and cutting. And he was so great at the modern-day roast. A bull charging into the ring. I was in for it.

I winced throughout the following: "Seriously, who gives a shit about Bob Saget? With your long neck, pointy beak, and granny glasses, you're like the Vlasic pickle stork."

It was hard to listen to but I loved every minute of it. After the roast, I decided I wanted to get to know Greg better and become friends with him. So I called him one night. He was at the Improv in L.A., and he answered his phone and said, "Bob, I'm standing next to a girl from Romania who wants to talk to you."

He handed her the phone and I spoke to a girl who spoke Russian-English. She told me her family was from Transylvania. I started to ask her questions about Dracula and lost her attention quickly, as she barely spoke English. Greg kept feeding her lines, trying to get her to ask me questions about *Full House*.

She didn't know what he was talking about. I heard him laughing in the background, relishing that she knew nothing of the show and had no idea who I was. He made her say to me, repeating after him, "I have no idea who you are." Then he grabbed the phone back, laughing at the "cellular roasting" he had just accomplished. We said we'd talk again soon and maybe go out to lunch sometime. He died about a month later. Like with George Carlin, I think he wanted to avoid lunch with me that badly. Rest in peace, Greg Giraldo.

As the taping went on, I was able to sit back and even started to enjoy myself for the couple hours it took to complete shooting it. It helped that most of the people doing the roasting were my friends. Norm MacDonald. He is one of the funniest people I have ever known. Norm and I spoke a couple days before the roast. He said, "Saget, I can't roast my friends. I hate that kind of humor." He told me he was going to tell old jokes from a roaster's joke book from the 1940s.

I said, "Norm, I don't know, that's a funny choice, but if it's not going well maybe you should just arbitrarily curse." I told him how I was once at a charity roast at the Beverly Hills Hotel, and the comedian and Oscar-winning actor Red Buttons, who was great at roasts and a lovely man, was in the middle of telling some jokes and hadn't cursed for a while. After a couple minutes, he said, "And in case you missed it . . . *FUCK!!*" Red Buttons. Loved him.

Norm listened intently. He didn't really, I just thought that was a book-smart thing of me to say, and I know he's going to read this. He listened to me with great intent. No, that's not true either. He intended to listen to me.

Anyway, he politely declined my suggestion that he arbitrarily curse. He didn't want to do what everybody else did and just tell filthy jokes. What ended up happening with Norm's bit in the roast actually became a comedic point of contention for people who care about these things. He made me laugh the hardest, because the man works with no net.

Norm committed to the choice of telling old jokes from the 1940s joke book. Some of the audience was puzzled. But to me and to a lot of people, it was hilarious. I just watched and laughed throughout. Wasn't too hard to figure out. Someone wrote about Norm's performance that it was "some of the best anti-comedy ever heard."

Norm wrote the jokes down on individual cards and committed to telling them. "Bob, you have a lot of well-wishers here tonight. And a lot of them would like to throw you *down* one . . . A well . . . They wanna murder you in a *well*. Seems a little harsh, but . . . Apparently they want to *murder you in a well.* It says here on this card."

Then . . . "Bob has a beautiful face. Like a flower. Yeah, a cauliflower. No offense . . . but your face . . . Looks . . . like a collie-flower."

Then slightly later . . . "I hear you have hair on your chest, Bob, and uh . . . Well, lemme tell you something . . . That isn't your only resemblance to Rin Tin Tin . . . *You're a fuckin' dog face!*"

A few other memorable moments came from my friend Gilbert Gottfried, who said: "I watched Bob's last HBO special in hi-def. Because in order to enjoy it, you have to be either high or deaf."

And then there was the incredible Cloris Leachman, who said the line that traveled "virally"—which, as she conveyed, never used to mean anything in her time of acting and actually "doing the work" . . . The line was: "I'm not here to roast Bob Saget; I'm here to fuck John Stamos."

Then she followed with: "I'm an Academy Award winner. For the love of God, will someone punch me in the face so I can see some stars?!"

The only thing that made me uncomfortable that night was the amount of jokes about my friends Mary-Kate Olsen and Ashley Olsen. I have a big personal stake in my relationship with those two ladies. I love them and didn't really want them to be subjected to what ended up being a hazing beyond my naïve expectations. But what the fuck am I talking about, because they're smart and expected it.

Part me of felt bad and part of me knew that comedy comes first, famous people come second, and if you're getting roasted, you have to try not to be a pussy. Also the writers and producers had made it clear early on that there were no prisoners to be taken. Producers take prisoners all the time. They're called writers.

The final story I want to share from the roast is a dramatic one that put a very gloomy haze over the whole day of shooting. It's about my friend—damn, I use that term a lot, but what the fuck, I am blessed and have a lot of friends . . . It's about my friend Artie Lange.

Artie, who costarred with Norm in *Dirty Work*, was all set to fly to L.A. the day before the roast. He had been going through a rough time. We shot the roast late on a Sunday afternoon. That morning at nine-thirty I got a call from the producer, Joel Gallen, telling me that Artie had overdosed the night before. I said, "Oh my God, is he okay?"

Joel told me he thought so . . . and they were trying to get Artie on a private jet with a nurse to make it to Los Angeles on time for the taping.

Shortly after, I got another call from Joel, who said Artie *wasn't* going to make it out—he was going to be okay but we still needed to get someone to fill his spot. There was one dilemma . . . All the jokes that had been written for Artie were "big man" jokes—or as we say in the trade, "fat jokes."

I put on my producer head, which by definition means having no soul while you're in work mode, and asked, "Who do we get?"

Joel said, "It's Ralphie May or Steve Schirripa . . . or . . . who else . . . ?"

I recall saying something like, "This is terrible, Artie's sick and we're casting. This is a horrible business. Who do we replace him with?"

I called my buddy who came to be the backbone of the roasts on Comedy Central, Jeff Ross. I remember the conversation crystal clear-ish: "I just talked to Joel. Artie OD'd last night. We have to figure out who can take his place."

Without missing a beat Jeff responded (and he later confirmed to me that he was "part serious"), "Oh my God! What am I gonna do? I got ten minutes of fat jokes!"

It was his knee-jerk reaction to respond to tragedy with a joke. And I embellish it here for comedic purposes. We were both really upset about Artie. We fucking love him.

Then we talked it out and actually had to deal with the fact that we were both getting picked up in three hours to go to Warner Bros. to rehearse for the roast. There was only one thing to decide upon. I called Joel back and said the two words we both instantaneously agreed upon to get through this difficult moment . . . Jeff Garlin.

It was another case of "size matters." I'd known Garlin for twenty-plus years but we weren't really close. That changed the moment he did the roast. On the air he reminded me of something I'd said to him at the L.A. Improv the night we met. He said, "I've always liked you. I remember when we first met you asked me if I knew how dry my grandma's vagina was."

I must've said it. He has a razor-sharp memory. He and I have been good friends ever since the roast. He's a funny, complex and loving human being.

Comedy is a complex thing. They've always said, "Dying is easy, comedy is hard." I guess it depends on how you die and how funny you were.

Chapter 11

RELATIONSHIPS I'D RATHER NOT TALK ABOUT

The length of this chapter is dictated by the number of lawyers involved with this manuscript. I am not one to name names, much to the dismay of a large sector of our culture. I *am* of course a rehabilitating name-dropper, a condition I don't think there is a cure for. But to talk about lascivious things I've done and name the people involved is not morally something I am capable of.

I'll do my best though. I'm sure someone will say, "Bob, please tell that story where we got all fucked-up in Vegas and we were in that suite together and that one dancer wound up in your room and another dancer wound up in my room."

Sorry, Stamos, I'm not telling it! One of those girls owns a pet store she needs to protect, as well as her relationship with her boyfriend—so no, those kinds of stories are not going to be in this chapter! Oh wait—shit, what did I just do!? Truth be told, in the end "nothing happened," as guys in tenth grade say. Although it's possible Stamos shot B-roll that night.

But alas, as I near the end of this book, I am not currently in a romantic relationship. At this point in time, all of the significant and meaningful relationships I have been in have met their endings. And endings are as important as beginnings. I had to put a few of them down—or they had to put *me* down, which is why I put *them* down. People can be so petulant sometimes.

I have nothing negative to say about any relationship I have ever been in. Unless you've got a couple hours.

One thing we all share in life is that relationships are tough. Even if you're fortunate enough to be in a wonderful, long-lasting relationship, you know that it can be hard work at times. It amazes me that anyone is able to last more than two and a half years together. The famous term is *the seven-year itch*. I went out with a girl once and I ended up with a four-day itch. During a first date is not a bad time to mention that you're a carrier of some kind.

If you want a relationship to have any chance of lasting, you have to be really honest with your partner and tell them what you want. "What you really really want. I wanna, I wanna, I wanna." You have to be able to Spice Girls up your relationship. I'm not suggesting ever bringing a third party into your bedroom. I'm suggesting bringing an all-girl band from the nineties into your bedroom.

"If you wanna be my lover, you gotta get with my friends." The writing was right there on the wall in those lyrics. Nothing to decode.

I don't know if I've made it completely clear, so I'll reiterate it just once more—I am single at the time of this writing. Although I've been receiving some very hopeful texts. I still believe I can find someone who understands me. Isn't that the core of most good relationships? We just want to be understood. And we must also desire to *listen* to the other person. What's that like?

Another way to go is to look for someone who doesn't speak your language at all. A few years back I went to Ukraine to shoot a TV show pilot about helping guys get mail-order brides. That was the opposite experience. Not one woman understood me there. It was kind of a dream. I got the same kind of reaction that I get when a woman who speaks English listens to everything I say to her: blank stares.

I was amazed how many American men wanted to bring home a bride who spoke no English. On one hand I understand it, but then on the other hand, it's hard for me to relate; I've always been such a head-y person. Obviously not now, with this book and all. With therapy and counseling as tools to help a relationship work, communication is key. With two languages being spoken and neither person knowing the other's, you are reduced to hoping for good connected sex, and beyond that, a few good meals and perhaps enjoying puppet theater together. What have I been talking about . . . Sold.

Maybe Jim Cameron was right. An *Avatar* love relationship may be the perfect one. Communication can be best without words. Words are what mess everything up. Texting doesn't seem to be helping either. I'm looking for a woman with no thumbs. Also would rule out the possibility of her hitchhiking to get away from me.

Some of the best moments in every relationship I've ever had actually required *no* words. Maybe if I'd never spoken at all, painted my face blue, and just thrown in an "I see you" every couple days I'd be married right now. That would be a dream. I could say one of my lame jokes, like, "Honey, you're looking a bit blue in the face tonight." She would just stare at me with no response.

If there's one thing that tests a relationship more than anything else, it's kids. Kids change everything. It's hard to keep the romance alive through the years when you're raising kids. There are only so many dead bolts you can put on your bedroom door. Peepholes, security camera, electric fencing . . . I'm embellishing. I'd never put a peephole in my bedroom door. That's just creepy.

Then there's work and the strain it can put on a relationship. It's a vicious circle. I find that in my hardest-working periods my relationships take a hit—whereas when I'm in between projects, even though I'm always working, I'm more inclined to spend time seeing if this new relationship could be "the one."

There's that wonderful period that usually starts when you first meet someone and then miraculously it sustains itself. I haven't been so fortunate as to have that last for all time. "All time" is a bit dramatic. "All time" means you're with someone until the end of at least one of your lives. I think a lot of young girls do fantasize about being with their guy forever. But do they understand what that means? Till old age, till one day you're sitting on the couch with your man watching your favorite TV show—and his eye falls out. I'm ever the romantic.

But if you have found "the one" and you're both reading this together and you are in perfect sync, you are very lucky. Either you've both perfected denial or there is an unspoken agreement that one of you completely controls the other person—and they dig it.

I'm looking for my emotional and intellectual equal. Truthfully, I've stopped looking; I'm creating one with my own DNA in a lab. I've decided to make a female clone of myself rather than keep looking to meet someone. Because I listen. I've *heard* what all my past relationships were telling me. As we broke up, they all imparted upon me the same wisdom, all saying in their own way, "I wish the best for you." One of them said that by saying "go fuck yourself," but that was just her way of being playful.

Falling in love is the magic time in a relationship. We all love falling in love. It's fun. Everything's more fun when you're in love. Flowers, chocolates, expensive shoes, diamonds. Until women actually quote Marilyn Monroe's rendition of "Diamonds Are a Girl's Best Friend."

If someone's singing that to you every day in a happy positive voice, your radar should go off. You've just been told that you are not this girl's best friend. Diamonds are. Shoulda noted that when you saw her on Craigslist or JDate.

I think about relationships a lot. It frustrates me that people who fall in love, myself included, can't cultivate that love and let it grow. I once said to a good friend of mine, "I'm fifty percent responsible in my relationships." His reply was, "No, each one of us is one hundred percent responsible." He's right. You can't blame anyone. Because you were there too. A'ight, I hear you, "it was all my fault."

I wish it could all be that fun gooey shit it's supposed to be that fills us all with butterflies and gets our hormones happily raging. But I think the difficulty of modern-day relationships is also partly cultural. People get bored and let in a bunch of bullshit from our reality-show-driven culture and just give up.

Everybody wants everything *now*—like Veruca Salt in *Willy Wonka*: "I want it *now*!"—and if they're not getting what they think fills their bottomless well immediately, they flit off to a better offer.

I've never done that. When a relationship of mine ends, I need some time to be alone, get back to myself—move back in with my mother. Take her out to dinner: "Freud, party of two, please!"

I know this chapter may be causing blue balls in some of my homeboy fans who thought this was gonna be fifteen pages about pussy. What can I say? I'm not great when it comes to having a purely sexual relationship. Oh wait, they don't exist, do they? I am so looking forward to my eighties. I am gonna get laid so much in my eighties.

When I'm eighty-four all I'm gonna do is have sex. Dirty sweaty veiny old-people sex. With the most beautiful, highest-tech machines on the market. That's right, I got it all planned. It'll be the year 2040 and I'll have the hookup! I'll be getting me some old-man techno pussssayyy!!

Sorry, needed that outburst. Forget everything I just wrote. In 2040 I'd like to be spooning in bed with someone I love. Please submit your applications in double-spaced writing. John Stamos need not apply.

In today's culture, nobody wants to work on a relationship anymore. It was different for my parents and their generation. My parents couldn't afford to break up. Sixty-three years together.

When it comes to money, I think there are two situations where money helps keep a couple together: either they have *no* money and hence nowhere to go, or they have insane amounts of money and . . . hmm, actually, now I can't think of any circumstance where incredibly wealthy people have stayed together happily, but I know they must exist. I've seen them walking around in Louis Vuitton stores.

I don't mean to paint a negative picture of marriage and relationships. I mean to write about it. It's hard to find true and lasting love in this day and age. Our values are backward. I've known a lot of beautiful women who just wanna be with their hedge-fund guy who's buying a missile silo. And why not? I can't disagree with them. If I was a hot woman I'd . . . no, let me stop myself there—if I was a hot woman all I would do is stay home and masturbate all day. But that's just me.

Okay, now I am concerned, and rightfully so, that this could be perceived as misogynistic and coming from a place of nonresponsibility. I love women, I hold them up high. And then I look up their dresses. Cleansing breath.

I think I need to print a separate copy of this book for my kids and loved ones to read. I mean, an R-rated movie is not supposed to let people under seventeen in without parental supervision—but that's not enforced. Does anybody stop a twelve-year-old from reading this book? I don't think so. I think *Fifty Shades of Grey* may be in some libraries. If it is, it's probably never been returned.

I once cohosted *The View* and they had me interview the author of *Fifty Shades of Grey*, E. L. James. That was a mistake. I told her I couldn't put her book down because it was stuck to my hand. She laughed. And then after the show she took me to her dressing room, made me put on a one-piece zippered-up gimp suit, and hung me upside down until I succumbed. That's not true. That never happened. But I still have the butt plug she signed for me. That book is about a type of deviant but romantic relationship that I've never had—but if I had, it would definitely fall into this chapter.

I think now's another good time for a disclaimer. I'm venting a bit because I've sometimes felt burned in this arena of love. Like most people, I've had some negative times. I ended a couple relationships. And startling as it may seem, I've been broken up with a couple times. Even after a first date, someone's going to either get a second chance or get rejected. We've all been on both sides and both sides hurt. But enough about my vulva. Same joke, different private part. Pointless. Why can't I keep a relationship going with clever banter like that, right?

I've always let relationships last too long. Getting better at it. I'm a Taurus guy, not that there's full validity to that—but I just don't like to leave. I always want it to work. But when it doesn't any-more, people need to split. It's tricky. Tricky, tricky, tricky tricky tricky tricky tricky. Run-DMC knows what I'm talkin' about.

We learn from all of our relationships and we learn from life, from all the people we meet. I'm still learning. There are a lot of good people in the world. You just don't always feel it going to bars. Or parties. Or family functions. Or watching *The Bachelor*. I've only seen that show once, and I like that there's a rose in it. That's so romantic, to show some guy giving a girl a rose in front of ten million people.

I know there are a lot of good, smart, kind people out in the world. I see humankind's glass as being more than half-full. Though sometimes the water in the glass looks a little cloudy, with Sea-Monkeys floating in it. They're just brine shrimp, you know. Yikes, and my mother got them for me as "pets."

My problem as a modern-day human is that I sometimes can't take the materialism of it all, and how, more than ever, material things seem to have replaced a life of love and actual happiness. I mean, I get it, I like *stuff* too. I like traveling well. I'm a bit of a spoiled bitch, actually. Stuff's pretty and it's a fun distraction, and

I don't want to come across as a hypocrite—so there, I said it: I like nice stuff—and I cannot lie. You other brothers can't deny. I'm Sir Mixed-Up-a-Lot.

I love good fashion. I even like Louis . . . C.K. . . . . He's the best.

As for the other Louis, Louis V—it's fun to have nicely made stuff, but I don't want that stuff as much after I hear about it on a loop in a rap song. And am I wrong, or do all their zippers suck?

I'm fortunate I can sometimes buy nice things for someone I love. I just don't like feeling like I'm buying a car when all I'm doing is picking out a purse or a rolly bag. I trust I haven't lost any of your attention. I know how many of my fans go into a Louis store. "I seen 'em!"

I have another theory at this moment in time—a two-and-a-half-years relationship theory. That's how long my several relationships have lasted since I was divorced—back during Prohibition . . . The magic of falling in love happens—that part is the best. It's before you're both concerned with things like "Wait, this isn't gonna last forever? Fuck, not again."

I've often wished I could've frozen my relationships in the falling-in-love stage. Magically suspend that time and make it last for the whole thing. There should also be no option that your marriage could have an end point. But crap, it happens. It takes special people to somehow find each other and know, and continue to know, that they belong together. Forever. I love meeting people who have that precious gift of lifetime love. I meet less and less of them these days. I look for 'em. Couples in love. They're fun to be around. Usually for about an hour.

In my life, after a breakup, it makes it harder and harder to let yourself fall in love again. They do call it "falling." And when you fall, someone's supposed to catch you. But if you break up, the one person who should be there to catch you, your significant other, can't *be* that person. Because you're broken up. No one prepares you for that. Some people try to be friends after a breakup. But if it was a romantic breakup, you're just trying to follow a script that doesn't for me feel real; it's not organic.

Two and a half years. I envy people who are still together after many years. That's who I should dedicate this book to. To the guy who read this book and then gave it to his wife, and she read it and still doesn't hate me. Damn, I love that couple. Seriously, let's double. Well, it'll be just me and both you guys, but I got dinner, and who wants to go for ice cream after!?

Breakups are not fun and the worst part of every breakup I've had is how it involves my kids, as well as friends and family who are left in its wake. Okay, *that's* who I have to dedicate this book to. Everyone who's had to help me through the breakups and listen to my bullshit. I don't want to go through it again. So I'm just gonna sit here in this Jacuzzi and type for the next thirty years. Don't mind me. Add some carrots and potatoes, I'm gonna change my name to Stew. I think I heard that joke in third grade. "What do you call a leper in a Jacuzzi?" "Stew." Yeah, I heard leper jokes in third grade.

When I was married at twenty-six I never thought my marriage would end when I was forty-one. I thought it was going to last our whole lives. I know most of you have been through this stuff in some way, either directly or with a farm animal. I dunno, I just wanted to check again if you're still reading.

Things happen. Life happens. With three phenomenal daughters between us, my ex-wife and I have become friends. It wasn't always easy. It took a while. A lot of my friends, both male and female, people I greatly respect, still haven't been able to achieve that with their exes. Some had kids together and some didn't. What they didn't know until reading this book is that *I* am the biological father of all my friends' kids. That's not going to travel well.

It took years for my ex-wife and me to become friends. I am unfortunately not close with any of my other exes. I learned a lot from them and I appreciated our time together, and I send them all good wishes, but staying buddies with someone I was in love with is just not how I'm made. I can't just "act" in my real life and change roles at the flip of a coin: "Okay, we're not gonna live together—no more sex ever—and we're gonna date other people, but let's be *besties*! Pinkie swear, it'll be great!!"

For me, once it's over, it's over. Anyway, that's how I've been up to this point in my life as a Taurus alpha male. And I value everyone I've ever dated as a person. Well, almost everyone—there was this one girl who was part jackal . . . no, not gonna do that. That's a relationship I'd rather not talk about.

I also enjoy *not* being in a relationship, the time alone. It's fun sometimes to just "be" and work on yourself. But I do find it a dilemma that the only groceries I've had in the house this past month are bottled water and toilet paper. Maybe I should use it all to make a ten-foot papier-mâché head and stick it on my front lawn as a statement. Okay, I just creeped myself out again.

I don't know if you can tell, but I'm far from an expert on relationships. I know most of you think I got it down. But I do believe you can look at *all* the people you've been in relationships with as a sort of a linear composite—as one long relationship, with lots of ups and downs—that can teach you about yourself.

This would be a good time to have the rehab guy in *Half Baked* stand up and yell: "*Relationships?* Man, this is some *bullshit!*"

I'm just proud of myself I wrote a chapter about relationships and decided, as a person with a modicum of dignity, to leave out the back-alley sex and not name names.

I haven't brought up the term *soul mate* yet, because as much as part of me wants to believe in it, I find the whole idea to be something out of Hallmark, not based on reality. I've had this discussion with a lot of people. Romance, especially young romance, inspires this belief in something as idealistic and sweet as a soul mate. And I think it's a *nice* thing to believe in. It's definitely something I wish I wasn't as cynical about. All of my relationships were *sole* mates of mine though, because they loved their shoes so very much.

I'm so happy for the few couples I've met and known over the years who are still in love, still growing, and not afraid to speak their truth to each other. Theirs are the rare relationships that just seem to *work*.

I have friends in Santa Fe, Terran and Bari Lovewave—yes, those are their names—who've been together for over thirty years. They're funny, smart, and I guess you'd call them *new-age types*. They host a local show on Santa Fe public radio. And I've been friends with them for over thirty years. Met them at a comedy club in Houston. Stayed friends until now.

They're best friends and love each other in that way that makes you sometimes want to leave a room to give them their privacy. I mean, they are *very* romantic with each other. Had sex right on my dining room table. During Thanksgiving. With all of us eating around them, nonplussed. Obviously not true, it was during Passover. But fact is, they are together and happy, and I don't know enough couples who are.

It's so fun when you're in the groove with someone. You're best friends, you share everything, you celebrate the successes, you make each other feel better when one of you is down . . . and then some real tough times come up, as they do for everyone, and . . . one of you leaves. No, I meant to end with, " . . . and you get through those tough times."

For me, the beginning of a relationship is always filled with great humor. If you're a fifteen-year-old guy reading this, I'm not suggesting you meet someone and fart as loud as you can for them because that's what you find funny. That's a tenth-date hard laugh.

Again, if you're a fifteen-year-old guy reading this, I'm hoping this information doesn't bum you out. "Nice book, Bob, I can't wait to fall in love and then be miserable. Thanks, Danny Tanner!" Every time I hear that name a chill goes up my butthole.

Sigmund Freud said, "We are never so helplessly unhappy as when we lose love." But he also said, "Time spent with cats is never wasted," proving once again that it's all about the pussy. I'm allergic to cats, and apparently, at least in this past decade, allergic to pussy. If cats really are your problem, before you ask someone out, it helps to do a nice Benadryl/Viagra combo before the first date.

First dates . . . what are they? For some, they can be hopeful. They can be fun. They can also be a disaster. It's rough when you have a friend fix you up with someone and you take her to dinner and soon as the first course comes you're asked, "So are you thinking of having children again?" It's not an unusual question for a guy like me who already has kids.

I trust my answer isn't too snarky: "Right now I was hoping we'd just get through our beet salads." I hate being rude. But I also find it weird that people can only find comfort in *the plan*, as in: "Let's find out what 'the plan' is and then we can get on with this meal and see if I want to ever speak to you again."

I understand. Everyone's biological clock is ticking. No one wants to waste their time. And again, time is the most precious thing we have. That and a solid stool. I'm a true romantic.

I once knew a woman, someone I cared a lot about, who was a bit like that, wanted to know the plan, wanted everything in the order she'd fantasized that her whole life would follow. And she stuck to it. And that's valid. But it's tough to do because things in life happen that we aren't prepared for. Like sharting your pants.

She had every right to believe in "the plan" she wanted. We all do. And hers wasn't anything out of the ordinary: just to date a little, get engaged, plan the wedding, plan the pregnancies . . . and then plan my death, my funeral, and who she'd then spend the rest of her life with, a venture capitalist or a restaurant owner. That would be a hard choice for even me to make.

I wish happiness for everyone I've ever loved. Even the jackal.

If you find it challenging to be friends with exes, that's actually a testament to how strongly you felt toward them at one time. It means you didn't want to just shift roles and "act" a different way to keep them in your life.

The idea of being "friends with benefits" is the subject of many relationship comedies. I don't get it. Wish I did. Back in the day I tried, but I can't just have random sex. Unless you call or text me and tell me you want to. Then I'll be right there. No, I'm not made that way. Okay, I'm in the car.

Actually, I used to be more like that a few years after my 1997 divorce, around the turn of the century, in the year 2000. When Conan O'Brien was on NBC he used to do this bit that I loved and did with him called "In the Year 2000." That has nothing to do with relationships, but I just hadn't name-dropped in so long I was getting anxious.

One relationship I've always admired is that of Howard Stern and his wife Beth. She understands his brilliance, his craziness, and embraces it. Romance aside, just to be able to have a man/woman relationship in the world of comedy that's in sync like theirs is a feat in itself. I've also admired the friendship and working relationship of Howard and Robin Quivers. I used to go on Howard's show quite a bit while I went through the years of being married, then through getting divorced, then through different stages of dating. It's a scary show to do, because it's early in the morning, and he's brutally honest and so skilled at what he does. The personal part of life you may not want to hear about could end up being the featured subject for the day. "So, how bad *really* is your circumcision scar?"

Stamos told me that Howard and I have a lot in common: we both have three wonderful daughters, an ex-wife we were with for many years since we were young, then divorced, and Jewish parents who sound and feel like they were made from the same mold. Not that all Jewish parents have mold. John also said, "There's one main difference between you and Howard—he has a billion dollars and you do not."

I am fascinated by the way some rare fortunate people are able to find love once, and then it changes, or they lose that person, and then they are able to find love again and be even happier. Have a second life. I have faith I will one day find that love. And I know I will pay handsomely for it.

The several relationships I've had since my divorce lasted two to three years, with one to two years in between each one. When I do that math, I realize that I too, not unlike Edward James Olmos, am the Immortal. I am one hundred thirty-four years old, with the libido of a twenty-five-year-old man and the maturity of a nine-year-old boy. Not really—more like a thirteen-year-old boy, because that's when most male humans can reproduce. I sometimes think how much more fun my Bar Mitzvah could've been if it had ended with getting my girlfriend at the time pregnant. All I got was a bike and a new stereo record player.

Throughout all of my relationships, I can say that I've tried and also that I've succeeded. My marriage was a successful one. And I believe that every relationship that came after it was successful as well, in the sense that I've learned a lot from every person I've had long relationships with. And I trust they feel the same way.

But excluding my children, the most consistent relationship in my life, for better or worse, as fucked-up as this is to say, has always been my relationship with my work. The work is always there. Sometimes I'm at my most comfortable when I'm standing in front of an audience. Or I'm in front of or behind a camera. Or I'm laying on my back to be X-rayed.

Stand-up is an interesting relationship. Every time I take the stage and I pull the mic out, it's as if it's in slow motion. It just feels so important to me. Like King Arthur pulling the sword out of the stone. It's that moment when it's just you and the audience. The moment that says, "Hello, friends. Thanks for always being there." That's the beautiful thing about stand-up. If you're in a healthy place mentally, you can be lonely but you're not alone. If you're in the flow of it, stand-up *is* a relationship.

There have been times when I've been in a less healthy place in my life and I didn't want to be alone. I was afraid of living alone after I had some knee surgery and was recuperating at home, and I wondered to myself, "What if I fall in the house and have to call 911?" For a while there I was going to bed clean-shaven and dressed up with my hair combed perfectly—just in case I fell and had to call an ambulance. Gotta look good for the hospital entrance. Can't wear a baseball cap and sunglasses for something as important as a *TMZ* appearance.

Speaking of being in my home incapacitated, I must be honest about my situation at the moment . . . I've been writing this for a long time now, and, you may be shocked to know, not all in one sitting. Circling back to how this all began—this is tough to share and this is not a joke; this shit is real . . .

I believe my laptop has permanently cauterized my testicles. It's as if they are now encased in a tortoiseshell cover. I'm afraid of even moving the computer right now and seeing what my sac looks like. A similar feeling, I'd imagine, to what Luke Skywalker felt when he took off Darth Vader's helmet and exposed his father's fucked-up face. You wanted to look, but you also didn't want to. Oh, shit, I hope I didn't just spoil *Return of the Jedi* for you.

So now it should come as no surprise to you that one of my best relationships this past year—due to this book—has been with my laptop. And as you've been reading, it's not always a perfect thing. Sometimes, not unlike your significant other, it heats up, then it cools down . . . It goes to sleep . . . And then it wakes up. It can lose its memory . . . You get the metaphor. I heat up, I can't cool down. Abracadabra.

I actually went to buy a new laptop before the completion of this book. It had a nine-hour battery life and didn't need a fan, so it never heated up. Super light and cool.

I tried it for one day and returned it. This book could not be written without my older-school laptop providing the constant heat within my loins, motivating me. Waking up my nether regions. But I digress.

I wasn't going to talk in this book about losing my virginity, but it's come up recently, because my hymen grew back about six months ago. I can count the girls I came in contact with as a teenager on one hand. Exactly.

I had a girlfriend when I was thirteen and then another when I was seventeen, which is when I lost my virginity. I had no previous intention of sharing that information, except that my friend . . . drumroll . . . John Stamos did an Internet show for Yahoo! called *Losing It*, where he got me to talk about it.

The premise of his show was that he'd interview his friends about their losing-it stories. I was John's second. On the show. And not unlike this book, if it's on the Internet, it will live forever.

Which reminds me of the classic song "Forever" by Jesse and the Rippers, my favorite boy band ever. Oh my God, did you see them that time on *Late Night with Jimmy Fallon*? They were so good I peed myself. Mullets gone wild.

A'ight, I'm gonna start to wrap up this relationship rant. Everybody's done some things they're not proud of. Valentine's Day has always been a point of contention for me. Not the movie. I love Garry Marshall no matter what . . . I'm talking about the holiday.

Every year when it rolls around, it hits hard. Sometimes it's been the greatest day ever. Other times, not so good. Some call it a "Hallmark holiday." I looked up Valentine's Day on my source of sources, Wikipedia, and it said the following: "The most popular martyrology associated with Saint Valentine was that he was imprisoned for performing weddings for soldiers who were forbidden to marry and for ministering to Christians, who were persecuted under the Roman Empire." Eggs-actly.

That's what I'm talkin' about. Gotta love martyrdom. The idea of being *forced* to show your love to someone on a certain day doesn't seem right. I don't think love should be forced. Unless you're being paid handsomely for it.

Now I must refute the whole point I just made, because on that day that I'm waxing cynical about, I've also been in love. When that happens, due to the luck of the Irish, or some wonderful aligning of the planets, it's the shit. It all works: the flowers, the gifts, the universal pat on the back you get: "Good for you, you're in love, like you're supposed to be. Like the *rest* of us."

And hell, it was fun back when we were kids, when everyone exchanged Valentines and we passed out those little sugar-heart things we all rotted our teeth with. I remember being able to kiss the girls in class and they kissed me. Lucky I didn't get kid herpes when I was five. Dear Lord, tell me there isn't such a thing.

I used to have crushes on some of the girls on the kindergarten Hebrew school bus—again, I wasn't even Jewish, I just knew at five that the hot girls were on the short bus to Hebrew school.

Sorry, yes, I am a Jewish man through insertion, once removed. As I type this, I'm looking at a picture of my father smiling. I do not want to be sitting with my mother when she reads this. Hi, Mom.

The first girl I had a crush on was named Chrissy. To the best of my recollection I was in second grade. Like seven or eight years old. I wasn't held back but I was a precocious little weird thing. I was either really outgoing and always trying to get laughs and attention, or really shy and geeky. I know, you're surprised only that I was shy. I was also a bit of a dirty little kid. I know, surprise again.

I got in trouble one time for looking up Chrissy's dress. We were doing arts and crafts and there were eight kids to a table. We were using these little blunt scissors to cut construction paper with. So I kept pretending to drop the scissors under the table so I could look up Chrissy's dress.

The teacher figured out what I was up to and told me to stop. To the best of my recollection, I did. Wherever Chrissy is today, I send my apologies for doing something so sleazy. I never repeated that behavior in my life—holding a pair of blunt scissors.

I am aware there's a crossover between this chapter, "Relationships I'd Rather Not Talk About," and the earlier chapter "Things I Shouldn't Have Done." I suppose if I hadn't been raised Jewish, I'd be able to get all of this out in confession. But guilt is guilt. Honesty and truth can cut through guilt. And it helps to have a pair of blunt scissors.

When I was fifteen I lived in L.A. a couple years and fell in love with an older woman. She was sixteen. I invited her to Disneyland. She said no. I got *no* a lot.

The second girlfriend in my life, when I was seventeen, said yes. When I was seventeen it was a very good year . . . (*See:* Frank Sinatra.) We dated through the end of high school, through college, and off again and on again my first few years living out in L.A. Mostly on again. And then one night I was at the Comedy Store in La Jolla for the weekend. I was twenty-five. I was back at the comedy condo. And I was stoned. That's what you do at a comedy condo.

I called my girlfriend back east and proposed to her. She said "yes." And that, kids, once again, is the story of how I met your mother.

The relationships I'd rather not talk about are obviously all meaningful to me. I feel shitty notating them as plural. Breaking down the word itself—and we've all heard this one—it's a "relation" and it's compounded with a "ship"—which does makes sense when you think of two people staying afloat together for any length of time. It's a lovely well-intended metaphor.

Swept away for a few weeks—what used to be called *an affair*—or together for a lifetime. The ship can set sail and have a beautiful journey, it can hit rough waters, and it can sink . . . it can go down. Although going down can save many a relationship.

And sometimes the people on the upper decks go below to hook up with the people on the lower decks. "I'll never let go, Jack." Wait, she did let go, didn't she? And we all have had that same observation.

Right after I'd seen *Titanic* it came to mind and I spouted it soon after onstage—and I've heard it from and discussed it with many people since . . . Rose could've shared the door with Jack, right? If Leonardo DiCaprio had played a working stand-up comic, he would've asked for a piece of the door. Then Rose would've had to let him float for a while and the flash-forward could've ended with Rose as an old woman, not throwing the giant diamond into the ocean but taking it to a pawnshop and having to split its value with Jack in their impending divorce.

I think I just made one of my earlier points . . . If Jack hadn't drowned, the idea of him and Rose as an older couple getting divorced—as the end of that movie—is worse than death. After three hours, you don't want to see that great movie ending in divorce. Death is more satisfying. I can actually hear crickets outside as I'm writing this. The universe gives us all the answers.

A woman I had a good relationship with for a while helped teach me that "words matter." Especially ones with four letters. I'm a person who has always needed to learn to be careful what I say. And I can't stress this enough: "Be careful what you say."

And in the present state of things, be even more careful what you text. Texting can ruin your relationship. So can cheating on the other person. I'm not saying one thing leads to the other, but these days, if you've accidentally read your betrayer's texts, it does. Oh, so I *am* saying that.

In contradiction to what I've just said, a wise man I truly respect recently told me that "words mean very little." It's your actions behind them. You can say "I love you" to someone but we all know those words are not always connected to action. Or to feeling.

One of my biggest flaws is I can say "I love you" at the drop of a zipper. No, I did not just write that. I apologize. I love you.

A while back, I thought I'd just met the woman who was perfect for me. And I told her exactly what she wanted to hear—"Okay, two hundred dollars, fine." That's completely untrue. I have never paid for sex. I have only paid for everything leading up to sex . . . and everything that follows sex . . . but I'd rather not talk about it.

Chapter 12

FALLING UPWARD, OR WHAT IT'S LIKE TO BE LOVED AND HATED

I'm always amazed when I go to do stand-up dates and the ad in the paper says, "For Mature Audiences Only." Nothing could be more immature than my stand-up. It's all derived from the silly humor my dad instilled in me. Poop and penis jokes. I really should be billed in perpetuity as "For Immature Audiences Only." I'm in the process of evolving past that. Could take a while.

When you're a comedian you can have a tendency to focus on even just one negative person in the audience who doesn't laugh because "they're just not that into you." Not every comic is like this. The smart performer takes in the 99 percent of the people who are enjoying their work. I used to have more of the unhealthy neurotic performer gene. It's a really good thing to get past.

I always admired the strength and self-belief in the work of Jerry Seinfeld and Bill Cosby. They never gave energy to people who did not like what they do.

I wasted a lot of years caring if someone didn't find me funny.

There's nothing you can do about it. Well, there *is* something you can do about it, but I found out you're not allowed to pump laughing gas into the air-conditioning system.

If you put yourself out there, people are always gonna take swipes at you. But life's too short to waste it on the one guy in the audience with his arms folded who hates you before you even start.

I got interviewed about some article once that said I was the "best" and the "worst" comic alive. It wasn't even an article, just some blog. It's like how a news channel will do a split screen, that feels like self-parody, but it's *the news*—where two people are interviewed: One side has a well-known director of our national security and the other side has a militant rebel whom no one knew anything about until the news channel gave him half of a split screen. Getting on television gives nobodies instant power.

Everyone is entitled to their opinion. That's upsetting sometimes, isn't it? I'm a sensitive guy who isn't always able to hear a negative opinion. And if you don't dig what I do, I can still respect you. But I don't know how it propels me forward either. It's not a positive thing for me or, I think, for the person saying it. I can't do negative anymore.

It's common for people on TV to have someone walk up to them and say, "I saw you on television last night." And that's it. They say nothing else. Not that they liked you or they didn't like you. And then they just stand there and stare at you, waiting for your response. And they're usually drunk. I can't do drunk people anymore either.

I've figured out that a good response is, "Thanks . . . ???" And it's usually followed by my texting my friend, "Let's get outta here." But my friend is standing right next to me, so I could've just told him. I can't do negative drunk people while I'm texting anymore either.

But it all comes with the territory of being a performer. There's the good and the bad. For example, I've always loved performing for college audiences. A joke from my newest stand-up special was that college girls often run up to me effusively and say, "Oh my God, I grew up watching you." And I say, "Well, good, 'cause now you're gonna go down watching me."

That's just a joke. I've got three daughters and I can't date people younger than them. I'm not saying I don't, I'm saying I can't. The rule is, as an older man, it's supposedly appropriate for you to date a woman seven years older than your oldest—or maybe it's add up all your children's ages, divide the total by two, and add seven? I dunno, their cumulative age is over seventy. I do have one rule though now when it comes to women: I won't date anyone older than my mother.

I love college audiences because although as a group they may be collectively stoned, they are all in the mode of *receiving* information. They tend to be smarter and more open than the general audience. Although that does depend on what school you're at. If you're performing at Missionary Position Two-Year State Trade School College, you may be in for an audience with lower-skewing IQs. I wouldn't know, I've never performed there.

I'm particularly fortunate to have a younger following. And part of what makes that so special is being able to be a parent to them in my own way. I get to tell young guys in the audience to stop getting all fucked-up on drugs and booze, and of course to stop having sex with animals. The two things go hand in hand—if you're not fucked-up, likelihood is you won't have sex with animals. I'm hoping that if I put that in print, people will believe it to be true. But I also believe that if you have sex with animals, you are not reading this book. Because odds are, you cannot read.

On the flipside, when I do stand-up, I get to tell young girls to stop giving it up and being young hos. I don't think it works, but that's actually my motivation through whatever morphing of hero worship I receive. I may say some nasty things, but my aim is true. It really disturbs me when I play a university or a rock and roll venue and girls flash their boobs at me. It disturbs me because there are barricades and I can't cop a feel. That's not true, I wouldn't do it if I could. Even if I was Inspector Gadget and had extendable arms and could shoot my hands out real quick to touch a titty, I wouldn't do it. I'm a father. And I don't know where they've been.

Last year I played the music festival Bonnaroo and several large guys made the same move. I'm really not big on men flashing their tits at me. Or tattooing me onto their ass. Yes, it exists. I seen 'em.

Regarding the sex-with-animals thing, I've actually had some disturbing experiences when I've played a school—where the one guy who *has* possibly done something with a goat shouts out. And he's so stoned and drunk he thinks I'm speaking *just* to him, and winds up taking his shirt off and trying to rush the stage.

I've learned to curtail that kind of behavior somewhat. I expect one day I'll look down into the front row and see a dude sitting there with his arm around the prizewinning sheep. Yessir, yessir, three bags full.

Over the years, people have asked me, "Why have you chosen this style of comedy? Are you trying to shock people?" That always comes out of left field for me. I didn't choose for my comedy to be scatological, immature, and what some people call dirty.

I'm just here to entertain people and make them laugh. And I'm not trying to prove that I'm not clean-cut. I don't even understand the concept of that. My most recent special, *That's What I'm Talkin' About*, is, for whatever reason, less dirty than my previous one. I know, "Good for you, Bobby." Fist-bumps. Shaka, brah.

When *That Ain't Right* came out in 2007, Don Rickles said to me, "Bob, I just saw your last special. It was very good. You left out two *fuck*s." And he slapped me in the face. And then he kissed me. I love that man. He's an original. Don never cursed in his act, which is amazing because he was always so cutting.

It's so cool to see Don and his friend Bob Newhart and their wives out to dinner. Newhart has also been one of my favorite comedians over the years. Sometimes Don does this impression of me to Newhart, which is of course an honor, where he mimics me and pretends he's singing a song by me that represents my stand-up. I've never actually uttered these lyrics, but Don has done this routine so many times I feel like it's real. It goes like this . . .

First, he sums up my looks as a "Jewish Clark Kent" and then he sings the lyrics as he imagines my act to be: " . . . And the monkey fucked the dog and the dog fucked the monkey . . ." All the while, as he's singing this, he's miming me playing the guitar.

Don curses for me because he knows it makes me laugh, especially coming from him. I've actually never talked dirty to the man myself. I don't really talk dirty to anyone much anymore unless there are a lot of people around. That's not a very tough thing to figure out the psychology of.

It's a strange yin and yang, the two sides of my work that I'm known for. I'm actually four-sided. But I've been doing more cardio.

Honestly, I do a lot of things that aren't blue or dirty, but nowadays people only remember the blue. Someone will mention my name to someone else who knows nothing about my work and the word-on-the-street response I hear a lot is "You know that dad from *Full House*? I hear he's dirty." Oh man. What to do . . . What to do . . .

I love that so many different demographics know me for different things. I was at the Walter Reed Army Medical Center just outside of Washington, DC. I love going there whenever I'm performing in the Capital. It is always an honor to meet some of our servicemen and women.

Several years ago when I visited, a very cool soldier asked me to come over to him. I joined him. Then he got very serious. He was smiling and kind, but he was serious: "I got a problem with you, Bob . . . I sat down to watch a show on HBO with my nine-year-old boy and it was you doing your stand-up."

He went on to explain that his son had wanted to watch the dad from *Full House*. The solider told me that he wasn't paying attention at first because he saw me on the television and he didn't know the tone of my comedy. After a minute he turned around because he started to actually hear what I was saying.

I felt terrible about it and told him, "When you see me on TV and it's on cable, please, sir, turn off the sound. I look like I'm saying nice stuff when the sound's off."

I told him how bad I felt and then he grabbed me and laughed and said he was just messing with me. But he was serious too. I did feel bad about that—except I assume by now his son's probably watched the whole thing a few times with his friends online.

If you watch my stand-up with the sound muted, I'd like to think I look like someone you can trust. Like your dentist—or your proctologist. What's the rest of that joke—"They both reached into the guy at the same time and shook hands in the middle."

One thing that's not a lot of fun for anyone is to be told who you look like. It's never good, even if the famous people they say you look like may be very attractive in their own way. I'm certain when people are told they look like me, they don't always jump for joy. Someone somewhere probably has though. Nahh.

I've been told I bear a resemblance to the following individuals: Bill Nye the Science Guy, Anthony Weiner, Rick Santorum, and Stephen Colbert. The only one of those comparisons that makes me genuinely happy is Colbert. That makes me gleeful. I'd be honored to look in the mirror and see *his* reflection. And I'd much rather hear his words than my own. I'm not that self-loathing; I just have a huge man-crush on Stephen Colbert. Forget how much smarter he is than me. No, I mean it—forget it.

I don't do well with look-alike doppelganger comparisons. Another thing I don't do well with is haters. Some performers don't let these people get to them or even get into their consciousness. Others feed it and thrive on the hate. So weird. It's bad enough to read a bad review—which we all know is not a healthy thing to do . . . unless you write them.

The Internet has opened the door wide to the world of haters. I'm a viral kind of guy so I know that being on Twitter itself is just asking for it. But thankfully, I see a lot more lovers than haters. And the haters I get, if I happen to see them I block 'em. I just don't need to do negative anymore.

When you perform live, eventually you're going to make direct eye contact with that one guy in the audience with his arms folded staring back at you. But I process it differently now. Maybe I misread that guy. Maybe he was just cold or checking his armpits for sweat or just had a really bad day.

And the great thing is, if I ever need a counterpoint to the arms-folded guy, I can just go right to my Twitter account and read, "@bobsaget is my favorite person in this entire world."

And then at the last minute I can decide not to post it.

Conclusion

MISSIONARY STATEMENT

As I wrote this book, a lot of people asked me if I had a ghostwriter. The answer is yes. It was Ernest Hemingway. And my house is full of his ghost vomit and urine. Hemingway said something that helped me get through this, my first book: "There is nothing to writing. All you do is sit down at a typewriter and bleed."

Things are cyclical. As I finish this book, I am reminded of how it began—with a laptop on my crotch. Hemingway did not have that luxury. I have had the good fortune to warm my testicles up while I write. With a typewriter in his lap for an entire book, Mr. Hemingway would've been ruined. *For Whom the Balls Toll. To Have and to Have Not . . . Balls. The Old Man and His Crushed Balls.*

So before I close I want to share a quick, non-testicle story about a man in my life whom I miss. He was my friend, the famed comedy manager, producer, and author Bernie Brillstein. He managed a lot of special people, including Jim Henson and Lorne Michaels, to name two.

I was on a trip with four couples, all good friends. I was the fifth couple. One day as the sun set, Bernie and me, just the two of us, were in a Jacuzzi on a boat in the Caribbean—tough times. Well, for me emotionally it was. I was newly single. Again.

Bernie was a jolly man, almost a Jewish Santa Claus, with the loudest laugh full of bravado. When he thought something was funny, you knew. His reaction was loud. And he also had that old-school show business comedic sense that you just don't see any-more. I loved hanging out with him and asking him stories about his life and the biz.

So, we're in this Jacuzzi—and I don't remember what I said to him but he just started to laugh. And he kept laughing. After a few beats he looked at me and said, "You know, Bob, if you could do in your career what you just did in this Jacuzzi, you'd be set for life." And I said, "What, take a shit?"

Yes, that's the punch line, but the real takeaway for me was the memory of his laughing at that with the loudest laugh you could hear. Making him laugh that hard was a special moment. Cine-matically you'd cut to an extremely wide aerial shot looking down on the yacht and barely be able to make us out hundreds of feet below—but the laugh would be echoing for miles.

What sparked this book was my musings on death and com-edy. This is what came out. What I wanted to share were my feel-ings about how humor gets you through this life and through all the dark times. For me, it's occasionally irreverent and immature humor. But funny is funny.

Like my friend Rodney Dangerfield used to say, "It is what it is." As I was adding those words earlier in this book, I was inspired to call my friend David Permut, who was Rodney's dear friend as well. I don't call David that much—good friend that I am—and I called him on his cell, unblocked.

David answered the phone: "You're not going to believe this."

I said, "What did I do? Have one of those psychic moments that I'm always bragging I have?"

He continued: "Bob, I am standing at this moment on Rodney's star on the Hollywood Walk of Fame."

He'd had a meeting to go to and visited Rodney's star because he had a half hour to kill. He hadn't been there since the day he and I were there for the ceremony when Rodney got the star. The morning he got some "respect."

A moment of synchronicity like that tells me that everything is where it's supposed to be. We all have them; they give us chills and let us know we are truly in the present. The key is to remember the moments. Don't take them for granted.

I learned from everyone I treasure—my daughters, my parents, Don Rickles, all my friends and relatives who went through huge losses our entire childhoods—that humor, however you define it, gets us through the saddest of times.

That was never clearer to me than at my father's funeral. Everybody loved my dad. He was just funny. Kind, smart, and funny. And full of love. So it was appropriate that he was eulogized comedically.

First up was my uncle Jonah, my dad's brother-in-law. He gave a loving speech and talked of my dad's influence and how they watched out for each other. Then he spoke at length about "self-service meats," which of course was the business he and my dad were in. You can't beat meat.

When you lose someone close to you, you find out who your friends are. My uncle Jonah was followed by my life-chosen brothers Paul and Brad. What they said touched me to this day.

When my dad passed away, it was unexpected. Tragically, I was not in town when it happened. I was in New York that night on Conan O'Brien's show promoting the fake documentary I'd made, *Farce of the Penguins*. My dearest friend Brad had this to say at my dad's funeral:

"They say laughter is the best medicine. Well, not in this case. The last thing Ben was watching was Bob's direct-to-DVD movie, *Farce of the Penguins*. Ben's last words were, 'For the love of God, someone turn this thing off!'" Big laugh. Which is exactly what my dad would've wanted.

I closed. I had an "okay set." Did a tight twenty and cried in the appropriate spots. I loved that man so much. It's an amazing thing when your dad is your hero.

My dad went through a sea of deaths. The oldest of six, he buried his four younger brothers and four of his children. Yes, I was it.

His philosophy after grieving was to laugh. To try to bring some joy to others, because life is just so hard sometimes. Because it ends.

My father also had a huge amount of dignity. This Mark Twain quote sums up the way my father and mother felt about life: "Keep away from people who try to belittle your ambitions. Small people always do that, but the really great make you feel that you, too, can become great."

As crazy and dark as I would imagine some of these stories sounded, I am very proud of the life I have led so far. I have a lot of love in my life. And a lot of laughs. And I wish that for you all.

I wish that even for the guy in the audience with his arms folded.

Author's Note

As I was writing this book over the past year and a half,
I began noticing that some of the events and themes described
within—loved ones becoming ill and how comedy gets us
through our pain—were coming true yet again. How crazy that
I was basically living out many of the tragic moments from
the book, once more, as I was writing it. I found it ironic yet
also sweetly poignant that life goes in cycles. As the book
went to press, I lost my loving mother at the age of eighty-nine.
A beloved wife, mother, grandmother, aunt, and friend, she
touched countless lives through the generations and will always
be remembered. This is for you, Mom.

Dolly Saget, 1925–2014

About the Author

Bob Saget is a Grammy-nominated stand-up comedian, actor, and television host. It was his family-friendly roles as the sweetly neurotic Danny Tanner on *Full House* and as the original host of *America's Funniest Home Videos* that made Saget a household name, but it is his edgy stand-up routines, comedy specials, and appearances in *The Aristocrats* and *Entourage* that solidified his reputation as a true original with a dirty sense of humor and unique personality. Although he has been performing raunchy stand-up for over thirty years now, it was only after he shattered his family-friendly image with the film *The Aristocrats* that Americans truly got to see the other side of Bob Saget.